gluten free
and easy

Robyn Russell

MURDOCH BOOKS

First published in 2004 by Robyn Russell
This edition published in 2007 by Murdoch Books Pty Limited
www.murdochbooks.com.au

Murdoch Books Australia
Pier 8/9
23 Hickson Road
Millers Point NSW 2000
Phone: +61 (0) 2 8220 2000
Fax: +61 (0) 2 8220 2558

Murdoch Books UK Limited
Erico House, 6th Floor
93–99 Upper Richmond Road
Putney, London SW15 2TG
Phone: +44 (0) 20 8785 5995
Fax: +44 (0) 20 8785 5985

Chief Executive: Juliet Rogers
Publishing Director: Kay Scarlett

Photographer: Elizabeth Ginn
Art Director: Tania Simanowsky
Editors: Margaret McDonell and Kim Rowney
Production: Maiya Levitch

Text copyright © 2004 Robyn Russell
Photography copyright © 2004 Elizabeth Ginn

National Library of Australia Cataloguing-in-Publication data:
    Russell, Robyn, 1961-.
    Gluten free and easy
    New ed.
    Includes index.
    ISBN 978 1921 25940 1
    1. Gluten-free diet - Recipes. 2. Quick and easy
        cookery. I. Title.
    641.56318

Printed by 1010 Printing International Limited in 2007.
PRINTED IN CHINA.

IMPORTANT: Those who might be at risk from the effects
of salmonella poisoning (the elderly, pregnant women, young
children and those suffering from immune deficiency diseases)
should consult their doctor with any concerns about eating
raw eggs.

CONVERSION GUIDE: You may find cooking times vary
depending on the oven you are using. For fan-forced ovens,
as a general rule, set the oven temperature to 20°C (35°F)
lower than indicated in the recipe. We have used 20 ml
(4 teaspoon) tablespoon measures. If you are using a 15 ml
(3 teaspoon) tablespoon, for most recipes the difference will
not be noticeable. However, for recipes using baking powder,
gelatine, bicarbonate of soda (baking soda), small amounts
of flour and cornflour (cornstarch), add an extra teaspoon for
each tablespoon specified.

INTRODUCTION

Coeliac (pronounced see-ly-ak) disease is a condition in which the lining of the small intestine is damaged by gluten, a protein found in wheat, barley, oats and rye. People with coeliac disease become extremely sick if they eat gluten as the body reacts to it as a poison, leaving them with nausea, vomiting, diarrhoea and a severely damaged digestive tract that prevents them from properly absorbing the nutrients in food. Initially thought to be a disease of infancy, it is now recognized that a range of symptoms can present at any stage in life. A study in Western Australia has indicated the incidence of gluten intolerance may be as high as 1:84; genetics playing a significant role. There is no cure for coeliac disease but it is very effectively managed with a life-long adherence to a gluten free diet. Currently the Australian Coeliac Society has over 10,000 medically diagnosed members, but these numbers don't include those who avoid wheat, barley, oats and rye to help control allergies or those who simply feel better if they limit their intake of those grains.

When I was initially diagnosed as having coeliac disease over 10 years ago I visited all the local health food shops and bought everything I could find that had 'gluten free' written on it. That was great while I was so desperately unwell but once my health improved I became a little more choosy and quickly grew tired of the food on offer. When I looked around for cookbooks so I could make what I felt like eating, there didn't seem to be any that offered stylish, inviting recipes that I'd want to try, let alone serve up to guests. Usually lumped into the 'alternative' or 'hippie diet' category, the limited selection was either lacking photos and printed on cheap paper, or foreign publications with difficult terminology and imported price tags. Well no more! Here's a book that celebrates the diverse range of foods that we can eat, each recipe with a gorgeous photo by Libby Ginn.

I've also found that friends without coeliac disease — often fabulous cooks — were sometimes overwhelmed at the prospect of cooking for me. While this cookbook is suitable for those following a gluten free diet, it's also perfect for their friends and family who have no idea what to make when faced with a non-wheat eating guest.

I'm not a professional cook, just a hungry person with coeliac disease who likes to serve modern food that looks and tastes good. I've stopped spending hours trying to turn out the soft breads from the old days, and now concentrate on the many things that I can have.

Food should be a pleasure not an obsession, so I hope this book helps to dispel some of the anxiety associated with gluten free cooking. This book is a compilation of my favourite recipes, none of them are difficult and none of them scream 'special diet'. This is the food that I've served my family and friends over the last 10 years. **RR**

Rice flour blend

It seems that a combination of gluten free flours achieves the best results when replacing wheat flour. For over 10 years I've mixed this with that and then that with a bit more of this and concluded that witchcraft must also be involved. Eventually I came across a combination that I call **Rice flour blend**. It's quite versatile and can be substituted cup for cup for wheat flour.

ingredients
240 g (8½ oz/2 cups) white rice flour
105 g (3½ oz/²⁄₃ cup) potato starch
40 g (1½ oz/¹⁄₃ cup) tapioca flour

method
1 Mix all the ingredients thoroughly and store in a canister so that you've always got some on hand.

✽ All brands of white rice flour are not the same and will produce vastly different results in your baked goods. I only recommend the brand that is listed on my website, as this has a very fine texture and is light weight. It is available in the Asian food section of the supermarket.

✽ Xanthan gum or guar gum is added to baked goods to prevent crumbling and helps to keep them moist. Both products can be purchased at health food stores.

✽ Gluten free baking powder❖ is added as a raising agent. I prefer to use plain flour and add the baking powder as I go, to ensure that the baking powder is potent and evenly distributed. Two teaspoons of baking powder per cup of **Rice flour blend** makes self-raising flour.

✽ For a few recipes I use a commercially available gluten free plain (all-purpose) flour❖, which contains some soy flour and therefore bakes up a little heavier but stays moist a little longer.

✽ As a general rule, I use the **Rice flour blend** in recipes where I want a lighter finished product, which will be eaten the same day, and the commercial flour in recipes such as fruit or nut loaves that have a heavier texture anyway.

THROUGHOUT THIS BOOK

Throughout this book you'll see this symbol ❖ next to some ingredients. It means **BEWARE: this product is a potential source of gluten and the ingredients on the label should be carefully checked.** Or simply visit our website
www.glutenfreeandeasy.com
look up that ingredient and see exactly which brand we used and where we bought it. We'll keep the website up to date and change the details should a product's status change. For that reason it's probably best not to print out the brand list but just check back from time to time.

This in no way means that you can slack off!!!

As a person with coeliac disease you should always check ingredients on any commercial product that you intend to eat. The website will at least point you, and those cooking for you, in the right direction for where to start looking. If you know something that we don't, tell us and we'll spread the word via the website.

This is not a medical book and the information it contains should not replace any recommendations given to you by your doctor or professional dietitian. It's simply a guide to what has worked for me, and I hope that it will help you too. If you've been medically diagnosed with coeliac disease you'll find the Coeliac Society in your state to be a good resource centre.

GOOD MORNING

Pink porridge

ingredients
25 g (1 oz/¼ cup) rolled rice flakes,
    ground fine in a blender
125 ml (4 fl oz/½ cup) cranberry and
    raspberry juice
125 ml (4 fl oz/½ cup) rice milk❖
1 generous tablespoon apple
    and raspberry puree
pinch ground cinnamon or allspice

to serve
plain Greek style yoghurt
raspberries or sliced strawberries
sliced almonds

method
1 In a saucepan over a gentle heat stir the ground rice
    flakes, juice and rice milk until thick.
2 Remove the pan from the heat and stir through the fruit
    puree and cinnamon or allspice.
3 Place the porridge into a serving bowl and top with a
    dollop of yoghurt, some berries and almonds.

Serves 1

Pancakes with blueberries

ingredients

90 g (3¼ oz/½ cup) brown rice flour
60 g (2¼ oz/½ cup) white rice flour
1 teaspoon baking powder❖
½ teaspoon xanthan gum
¼ teaspoon salt
3 tablespoons golden syrup or honey
2 tablespoons canola oil
1 egg
125–185 ml (4–6 fl oz/½–¾ cup) milk
   or rice milk❖
1 generous teaspoon apple puree
¼ teaspoon natural vanilla extract

to serve
fresh blueberries and **Blueberry sauce**
pure maple syrup, optional

method

1 Sift all the dry ingredients into a bowl and mix well.

2 In a separate bowl place the golden syrup, oil, egg,
125 ml (4 fl oz/½ cup) of the milk, apple puree and vanilla
and mix with a hand blender until frothy.

3 Stir the wet ingredients into the dry, adding the rest of the
milk as needed to make a smooth pouring batter. Place
tablespoons of batter into a heated frying pan and cook
until bubbles appear on top. Flip the pancakes and cook
the other side.

4 Serve the pancakes with fresh blueberries and blueberry
sauce or that perennial favourite: pure maple syrup.

Makes about 12 pancakes

Apple and raspberry quick bread

The apple in this bread helps keep it fresh or it can be gently toasted under the grill (broiler).

ingredients

165 g (5¾ oz/1½ cups) commercial gluten free plain (all-purpose) flour❖, measured after sifting
1½ teaspoons baking powder❖
½ teaspoon bicarbonate of soda (baking soda)
½ teaspoon xanthan gum
1 teaspoon ground cinnamon
¼ teaspoon allspice
¼ teaspoon freshly grated nutmeg
¼ teaspoon salt
95 g (3½ oz/½ cup) soft brown sugar
80 ml (2½ fl oz/⅓ cup) canola oil
65 g (2¼ oz/¼ cup) apple puree
2 large eggs
60 g (2¼ oz/½ cup) grated apple, such as Fuji
60 g (2¼ oz/½ cup) raspberries

topping

1 tablespoon caster (superfine) sugar
¼ teaspoon ground cinnamon
¼ teaspoon freshly grated nutmeg

method

1 Preheat oven to 180°C (350°F/Gas 4).
2 Grease and line the bases of two mini loaf tins, 11 cm x 8 cm (4¼ in x 3¼ in).
3 To make the topping, combine the sugar, cinnamon and nutmeg and set aside.
4 Sift the flour, baking powder, bicarbonate of soda, xanthan gum, spices and salt into a bowl. Stir until well combined.
5 In a separate bowl whisk together the sugar, oil, apple puree and eggs until frothy. Add to the dry ingredients and mix well. Fold in the grated apple until evenly distributed then gently stir through the raspberries.
6 Divide the batter between the prepared tins, sprinkle the topping over and bake for 25–30 minutes or until the loaves are cooked through.
7 Allow the loaves to set in their tins for a few minutes then turn out to cool on a wire rack.

Makes 2 loaves

Apple and raspberry muffins

This mixture also bakes up well as about eight generous muffins, but reduce the cooking time to 20 minutes.

Two fruit and yoghurt protein smoothie

Freeze ripe fruit chunks when they're in season to add straight to the blender — better than ice cubes.

ingredients

1 ripe banana, cut into chunks
35 g (1 ¼ oz/¼ cup) strawberries
60 g (2 ¼ oz/¼ cup) plain Greek style
  yoghurt
1 tablespoon protein powder❖
250 ml (9 fl oz/1 cup) cold rice milk❖
  or soy milk❖

method

1 Puree all ingredients in a blender,
   mix well, then pour into a tall,
   chilled glass to serve.

Serves 1

variations

❋ Apricot and banana
❋ Kiwi fruit and blueberry
❋ Peach and strawberry
❋ Rockmelon and raspberry
❋ Raspberry and banana
❋ Blueberry, raspberry and strawberry
❋ Passionfruit and mango
❋ Peach and banana
❋ For a chocolate fix, skip the fruit
   and add 1 generous teaspoon of
   hazelnut and chocolate spread❖.

Mashed potato cakes

These delicious potato cakes make a wonderful breakfast served with fried tomatoes, bacon and eggs.

ingredients

800 g (1 lb 12 oz) all-purpose
  potatoes, peeled and diced
40 g (1½ oz/½ cup) finely grated
  Jarlsberg cheese
60 g (2¼ oz/¼ cup) sour cream
1 egg, lightly beaten
2 tablespoons chopped chives
1 teaspoon sea salt
1 spring onion (scallion), chopped
extra sea salt and ground black
  pepper, to taste

method

1 Preheat oven to 200°C (400°F/
  Gas 6).
2 Grease a non-stick baking tray.
3 Steam the potatoes until soft then
  mash with a vegetable ricer or mill.
  In a large bowl mix the potatoes,
  cheese, sour cream, egg, chives,
  salt and spring onion. Season with
  extra salt and pepper. Using wet
  hands, form into eight flat patties.
4 Place the patties on the tray and
  spray the tops lightly with a little
  cooking oil. Bake for 15 minutes
  until browned on the bottom then
  flip over, flatten gently and bake
  until well browned.

Makes 8–10 patties

Baked eggs

ingredients

1 teaspoon olive oil

1 leek, white part only, washed well
and finely sliced

¼ teaspoon crushed garlic

100 g (3½ oz) fresh ham, diced

600 g (1 lb 5 oz) English spinach leaves,
washed, drained and shredded

2 tablespoons finely grated parmesan
cheese

salt and pepper, to taste

4 large eggs

method

1 Preheat oven to 170°C (325°F/Gas 3).

2 Grease four shallow ovenproof dishes or ramekins.

3 Heat the olive oil in a frying pan and sauté the leek until
soft. Add the garlic, ham and spinach and stir until the
spinach starts to wilt. Remove from the heat and drain off
the excess moisture. Stir through the parmesan cheese
and season with salt and pepper.

4 Divide the mixture among the baking dishes, make a little
hollow in the spinach and crack one egg into each.

5 Bake until done to your liking, about 10 minutes for soft
yolks, 15 minutes for set yolks.

Serves 4

Corned beef hash

ingredients

1 large onion, diced
1 teaspoon crushed garlic
3 tablespoons olive oil
1 small red capsicum (pepper), diced
1 small yellow capsicum (pepper), diced
1 large all-purpose potato, chopped
    into small dice
400 g (14 oz) home-cooked corned beef
5 g (⅛ oz/¼ cup) Italian (flat-leaf) parsley
100 g (3½ oz/½ cup) tinned corn kernels
¼ teaspoon cayenne pepper
½ teaspoon ground black pepper
salt, to taste

to serve

4 large fried eggs

method

1 In a large saucepan or frying pan sauté the onion and garlic in the olive oil until soft. Stir in the red and yellow capsicums then cover the pan with a lid and leave to soften for a few minutes.

2 Steam or microwave the diced potato until cooked then add to the frying pan.

3 In a food processor pulse the corned beef and parsley to small pieces then add to the vegetables. Add the corn, cayenne pepper, black pepper and salt, to taste and stir until heated through. Add another tablespoon or two of olive oil if the mixture seems a little dry.

4 To serve, place a generous pile of hash on individual plates and serve with fried eggs on the side.

Serves 4

Baked adzuki beans

This recipe makes a fairly generous pot of beans but they keep well and make a great snack. The blended sauce can be prepared ahead of time and left to mellow, or it can be frozen and the beans added at serving time.

ingredients

2 tablespoons olive oil

1 large onion, finely diced

½ teaspoon crushed garlic

4 rindless bacon slices, finely diced

700 g (1 lb 9 oz) bottle tomato passata
   (pureed tomatoes)

2 tablespoons tomato paste
   (concentrated puree)

250 ml (9 fl oz/1 cup) chicken stock✣

1 teaspoon soft brown sugar

2 tablespoons pure maple syrup

1 teaspoon dijon mustard✣

1 teaspoon sea salt, or to taste

2 x 425 g (15 oz) tins adzuki beans,
   rinsed and drained

2 tablespoons chopped flat-leaf (Italian)
   parsley

1 teaspoon chilli flakes, optional

method

1 Heat the olive oil in a saucepan, add the onion and garlic and cook until soft. Add the bacon and cook until lightly browned then add the tomato passata, tomato paste, stock, brown sugar, maple syrup, mustard and sea salt. Simmer, covered, for 10 minutes or until the sauce has thickened, stirring occasionally to prevent burning.

2 Puree the sauce in a blender then return to the saucepan and stir in the beans, parsley and chilli.

3 Heat through, season to taste with more salt and serve.

Serves 6–8

Chilli cheddar cornbread

This cornbread pairs well with dishes such as **Piperade** or **Baked adzuki beans**. Served as a side dish for soup, it makes a substantial lunch.

ingredients

140 g (5 oz/1 cup) **Rice flour blend**

175 g (6 oz/1 cup) fine polenta

2 teaspoons baking powder❖

½ teaspoon bicarbonate of soda (baking soda)

1 teaspoon sea salt

170 ml (5½ fl oz/⅔ cup) buttermilk

2 large eggs plus 1 egg white, lightly beaten

160 g (5½ oz/⅔ cup) tinned creamed corn

125 g (4½ oz/1 cup) finely grated mature cheddar cheese

3 spring onions (scallions), finely sliced

1 red or green cayenne chilli, seeded and finely chopped

method

1 Preheat oven to 200°C (400°F/Gas 6).

2 Grease and line a 21 cm (8¼ in) square baking tin.

3 In a bowl sift together the flour, polenta, baking powder, bicarbonate of soda and salt. Mix until well combined.

4 In a separate bowl mix together the buttermilk and eggs and stir into the flour mixture.

5 Fold in the creamed corn, cheese, spring onions and chilli and stir until just combined.

6 Spoon into the prepared tin and bake for 30 minutes or until lightly browned. Allow to firm up in the tin for a few minutes then turn out to cool on a wire rack.

7 Serve chilli cornbread cut into squares, or split the slices in half, toast under the grill (broiler) and spread with butter.

Serves 4–6

Salmon kedgeree

ingredients

155 g (5½ oz/¾ cup) wild blend rice
1 tablespoon mustard seed oil or olive oil
½ teaspoon dried turmeric
2 leeks, white part only, washed well
    and sliced
210 g (7½ oz) tin red salmon, drained
    and broken into pieces
1 celery stalk, finely diced
2 hard-boiled eggs, sliced
2 tablespoons finely chopped flat-leaf
    (Italian) parsley
2 tablespoons lemon juice
salt and pepper, to taste

to serve

plain Greek style yoghurt
chopped spring onions (scallions)

method

1 Bring 500 ml (17 fl oz/2 cups) salted water to the boil, add the rice then cover and simmer until all the liquid has been absorbed, about 12 minutes.

2 Heat the oil in a frying pan, add the turmeric and sliced leeks and cook until the leeks are tender. Stir in the cooked rice, salmon, celery, most of the egg slices, parsley and lemon juice and toss to combine. Season to taste with salt and pepper.

3 To serve, spoon some kedgeree onto a plate, top with a generous dollop of yoghurt, some chopped spring onions and a few reserved egg slices.

Serves 4

Piperade

This Basque style dish is one of those handy things to have in the refrigerator as it mellows well and is quite versatile. Traditionally made with capsicums and tomatoes, I've added some potato to make it more of a stand-alone dish than just a sauce. Here it is served as a spicy brunch but it pairs equally well with garlicky chevapi sausages✤, barbecued tuna or chicken.

ingredients

1 large onion, diced
1 red capsicum (pepper), diced
1 yellow capsicum (pepper), diced
1 large all-purpose potato, diced
1 tablespoon olive oil
½ teaspoon crushed garlic
½ teaspoon sweet paprika
¼ teaspoon cayenne pepper, or to taste, optional
800 g (1 lb 12 oz) tin chopped tomatoes with juice
2 tablespoons chopped flat-leaf (Italian) parsley
salt and pepper, to taste

to serve

freshly grated parmesan cheese
scrambled eggs
freshly sliced ham from the bone

method

1 In a large saucepan cook the onion, red and yellow capsicums and potato in olive oil until softened. Add the garlic, paprika and cayenne pepper and cook for a minute longer, stirring.
2 Stir in the undrained tomatoes and simmer, uncovered, until the sauce is rich and thick and the vegetables are cooked through. Stir through the parsley and season with salt and pepper.
3 Place a generous spoonful of piperade onto warmed serving plates and top with grated parmesan cheese.
4 Serve with scrambled eggs and fresh ham.

Serves 4

French potato salad

This makes a nice change from the usual dairy-based potato salads, and any leftovers are great the next day with some drained, oil-packed tuna and cherry tomatoes.

ingredients

1 kg (2 lb 4 oz) all-purpose
  potatoes, unpeeled, sliced
3 tablespoons olive oil
1 teaspoon white wine vinegar
1 teaspoon dijon mustard❖
½ teaspoon salt
7 g (¼ oz/¼ cup) chopped Italian
  (flat-leaf) parsley
1 spring onion (scallion), chopped
1 tablespoon chopped basil

method

1 Steam the sliced potatoes over salted boiling water until just tender. Rinse and drain and allow to cool a little.

2 In a glass jar with a lid combine the olive oil, vinegar, mustard and salt and shake well.

3 Transfer the poatoes to a serving bowl and pour the dressing over the still-warm potatoes and toss gently to coat.

4 Cool a little more then stir in the parsley, spring onion and basil and season with salt and pepper.

5 Serve warm or at room temperature.

Serves 4–6 as a side dish

Gado-gado

This Indonesian chicken and vegetable salad uses **Satay sauce** as a dressing. Any vegetables can be used and rice noodles✣ can be substituted for the potatoes.

ingredients

2 all-purpose potatoes (such as desiree), unpeeled, sliced
4 small boneless, skinless chicken breasts
400 ml (14 fl oz) tin coconut milk
45 g (1½ oz/1 cup) shredded Chinese cabbage
1 large carrot, sliced into ribbons with a vegetable peeler
125 g (4½ oz/1 cup) green beans cut into 3 cm (1¼ in) lengths
1 Lebanese (short) cucumber, sliced into ribbons with a vegetable peeler
8 baby corn, quartered
1 handful snow pea (mangetout) sprouts
125 g (4½ oz/½ cup) **Satay sauce**, thinned with a little water, for dressing
2 hard-boiled eggs, quartered
2 spring onions (scallions), chopped

method

1 Steam the sliced potatoes over salted boiling water until just tender. Rinse and drain and allow to cool.

2 Place the chicken and coconut milk into a large saucepan, adding water if necessary to cover the chicken. Cover the pan and gently poach the chicken over medium heat until cooked through. Cool in the poaching liquid and when cold shred the chicken into small pieces.

3 Arrange the vegetables on a large serving plate and place the chicken on top. Drizzle with half the **Satay sauce** then top with the hard-boiled eggs and chopped spring onions. Pass the remaining **Satay sauce** separately.

Serves 4

Quinoa tabouleh

Quinoa, pronounced 'keenwa', contains more protein than any other grain, is very light and has a lovely nutty flavour. Available from health food stores and in the health food aisles of larger supermarkets, it's as easy to cook as rice and makes a great alternative to couscous, another no-no.

ingredients

100 g (3½ oz/½ cup) quinoa
250 ml (9 fl oz/1 cup) chicken stock❖
½ teaspoon salt
100 g (3½ oz) semi-dried (sun-blushed) tomatoes, diced
1 Lebanese (short) cucumber, diced
6 spring onions (scallions), finely chopped
30 g (1 oz/1 cup) finely chopped flat-leaf (Italian) parsley
3 tablespoons olive oil or the reserved oil from the tomatoes
3 tablespoons lemon juice
¼ teaspoon crushed garlic
salt and pepper, to taste

method

1 Place the quinoa in a sieve and wash well under running water then drain. Toast the quinoa in a hot dry frying pan until fragrant.

2 In a saucepan bring the chicken stock to the boil, stir in the quinoa and salt and simmer, covered, until all the stock is absorbed, about 12 minutes. Fluff with a fork and leave covered in the pan for another 10 minutes. Cover and refrigerate until needed.

3 In a large bowl place the tomatoes, cucumber, spring onions and parsley and toss to combine. Stir in as much of the quinoa as needed to give a balanced look to the salad.

4 In a glass jar with a lid combine the olive oil, lemon juice, garlic and salt and pepper. Shake well. Pour over the salad, toss to coat and serve.

Serves 4

Quinoa, eggplant and chickpea salad

ingredients

250 ml (9 fl oz/1 cup) water
100 g (3½ oz/½ cup) quinoa
olive oil
1 small onion, chopped
1 teaspoon crushed garlic
2 teaspoons ground coriander
½ teaspoon ground cinnamon
½ teaspoon ground cardamom
½ teaspoon garam masala
1 large eggplant (aubergine), chopped
400 g (14 oz) tin chickpeas, drained
   and rinsed
25 g (1 oz/½ cup) chopped coriander
   (cilantro) leaves
15 g (½ oz/½ cup) chopped flat-leaf
   (Italian) parsley
salt, to taste

dressing

125 g (4½ oz/½ cup) plain Greek style
   yoghurt
2 tablespoons chopped mint
1 teaspoon ground cumin

method

1 Place the quinoa in a sieve and wash well under running water then drain. Toast the quinoa in a hot dry frying pan until fragrant.

2 Pour the water into a saucepan, bring to the boil and stir in the quinoa. Simmer, covered, for about 12 minutes until soft. Remove from the heat, fluff with a fork and leave covered in the pan for another 10 minutes.

3 Heat the olive oil in a frying pan and fry the onion gently until very soft then add the garlic and ground spices and cook for a few more minutes. Add the eggplant to the pan and cook, stirring, until golden, adding extra oil if necessary. Add the chickpeas and stir until heated through. Remove the pan from the heat and stir through the coriander, parsley and quinoa. Season with salt.

4 To make the dressing, in a bowl combine the yoghurt, mint and cumin.

5 Serve the salad warm or at room temperature drizzled with dressing.

Serves 4

Greek salad

ingredients

250 g (9 oz) roma (plum) tomatoes, cut
    into wedges
150 g (5½ oz) Lebanese (short) cucum-
    bers, halved lengthways and sliced
1 cos (romaine) lettuce, shredded
155 g (5½ oz/1 cup) pitted black olives
1 red onion, finely diced
4 spring onions (scallions), chopped
2 tablespoons chopped flat-leaf (Italian)
    parsley
100 g (3½ oz) feta cheese❖, chopped

dressing

2 tablespoons extra virgin olive oil
1 tablespoon white wine vinegar
1 tablespoon lemon juice
½ teaspoon dried oregano
¼ teaspoon crushed garlic
salt, to taste

method

1 Combine all the salad ingredients, except the feta, in a
serving bowl and toss.
2 Combine all the dressing ingredients in a glass jar with
a lid and shake well. Pour the dressing over the salad,
toss to coat and top with the feta cheese.

Serves 4

Chicken and wild rice salad

This salad can be made ahead as the flavour improves with a little time.

ingredients

50 g (1¾ oz/½ cup) pecan nuts
250 ml (9 fl oz/1 cup) water
100 g (3½ oz/½ cup) wild blend rice
½ teaspoon salt
1 large double boneless, skinless
   chicken breast
1 teaspoon black peppercorns
1 onion, sliced
200 g (7 oz/1 cup) tinned corn kernels
1 small red onion, finely diced
2 tablespoons currants
3 tablespoons chopped flat-leaf (Italian)
   parsley
80 ml (2½ fl oz/⅓ cup) orange juice
125 ml (4 fl oz/½ cup) macadamia oil
2 tablespoons white wine vinegar
salt and pepper, to taste

method

1 Roast the pecans in a hot dry frying pan for a few minutes, stirring to brown evenly. Cool and roughly chop.

2 In a saucepan bring the water, wild rice and salt to the boil, reduce the heat, cover the pan and simmer for 15 minutes. Remove from the heat, fluff the rice with a fork and leave covered for 10 minutes. Refrigerate until needed.

3 Place the chicken in a saucepan with the peppercorns and sliced onion and enough water to cover the chicken. Cover the pan, bring to a very gentle simmer and poach the chicken until cooked through. Cool the chicken in the poaching liquid then remove and chop into smaller pieces.

4 Combine the chicken, pecans, rice, corn, red onion, currants and parsley in a bowl.

5 Mix together the orange juice, macadamia oil and vinegar and pour over the salad. Toss to combine then season with salt and pepper. Cover and refrigerate overnight for the flavours to develop.

6 Bring the salad to room temperature to serve.

Serves 4

Tuna salad niçoise

ingredients

250 g (9 oz) green beans, blanched

170 g (6 oz/1 cup) halved cherry
tomatoes

170 g (6 oz/1 cup) halved yellow
teardrop tomatoes

120 g (4¼ oz/½ cup) sliced roasted
capsicum (pepper)

200 g (7 oz) tin cannellini beans, drained
and rinsed

80 g (2¾ oz/½ cup) pitted small
black olives

185 g (6½ oz) tin tuna packed in oil,
drained

½ small red onion, finely diced

4 hard-boiled eggs, quartered

salt and ground black pepper, to taste

dressing

2 tablespoons olive oil

2 teaspoons red or white wine vinegar

½ teaspoon chopped basil

method

1 In a large bowl combine all the salad ingredients except
the hard-boiled eggs.

2 Combine the dressing ingredients in a glass jar with a lid
and shake well.

3 Pour the dressing over the salad. Toss to combine,
season with salt and pepper and then gently add the
hard-boiled eggs.

Serves 4

Turkey cobb salad with tahini vinaigrette

ingredients

50 g (1¾ oz/1 cup) baby English spinach leaves

1 small cos (romaine) lettuce, shredded

300 g (10½ oz) cooked turkey, chopped

2 ripe avocados, chopped and tossed with a little lemon juice

3 roma (plum) tomatoes, seeded and chopped

6 rindless bacon slices, cooked and crumbled

60 g (2¼ oz/½ cup) finely sliced Jarlsberg cheese

110 g (3¾ oz/¾ cup) tinned chickpeas, drained and rinsed

2 hard-boiled eggs, chopped

30 g (1 oz/¼ cup) pitted black olives, sliced

1 carrot, sliced into ribbons with a vegetable peeler

method

1 Combine the spinach and lettuce in a bowl and toss in a little **Tahini vinaigrette**. Divide among individual serving plates and arrange the rest of the ingredients on top. Drizzle with a little more dressing and serve.

Serves 4

TAHINI VINAIGRETTE

In a glass jar with a lid combine 1 tablespoon tahini, 1 tablespoon lemon juice, 2 teaspoons white wine vinegar, 1 teaspoon grain mustard❖, 80 ml (2½ fl oz/⅓ cup) olive oil and 2 tablespoons water. Shake well to combine and season with salt and pepper or a little sugar. Add more water if necessary to thin the vinaigrette to the desired consistency.

Tahini coleslaw

Core and shred ¼ small red cabbage and ¼ small green cabbage. In a large bowl toss the cabbage, 1 coarsely grated carrot, 20 g (¾ oz/½ cup) shredded baby English spinach leaves, 3 chopped spring onions (scallions) and 2 tablespoons chopped flat-leaf (Italian) parsley. Pour the **Tahini vinaigrette** over the coleslaw, toss to coat and leave to sit for an hour or so for flavours to develop.

Minestrone

The prosciutto in this soup really makes all the difference — don't use bacon as the flavour is too strong.

ingredients

1 onion, sliced
1 tablespoon olive oil
½ teaspoon crushed garlic
1 celery stalk, diced
2 carrots, diced
80 g (2¾ oz) prosciutto, diced
1 litre (35 fl oz/4 cups) water
2 large tomatoes, peeled and chopped
piece of parmesan rind
155 g (5½ oz/1 cup) shelled peas
75 g (2½ oz/1 cup) shredded cabbage
125 g (4½ oz/1 cup) chopped green
   beans
300 g (10½ oz) tin cannellini beans or
   small butter beans, drained and rinsed

to serve

1 tablespoon finely chopped basil
finely grated parmesan cheese

method

1 In a large saucepan sauté the onion in the olive oil until translucent then add the garlic, celery, carrots and prosciutto. Cook, stirring, until the prosciutto is lightly browned then add the water, tomatoes and parmesan rind. Cover the saucepan and bring to the boil then reduce the heat to a simmer.

2 Add the peas, cabbage, green beans and cannellini beans to the pan and simmer, uncovered, for a further 10 minutes. The soup should be thick with vegetables but add more water if you prefer. Leave the minestrone to mellow for a few hours or overnight, covered, in the refrigerator.

3 To serve, reheat the soup and discard the parmesan rind then stir through the basil and garnish with grated parmesan cheese.

Serves 4

Gazpacho

ingredients
500 ml (17 fl oz) tin V8 juice
3 roma (plum) tomatoes, seeded
1 Lebanese (short) or ½ telegraph (long)
  cucumber, peeled, seeded and
  chopped
¼ red onion, chopped
½ small red capsicum (pepper), diced
1 tablespoon flat-leaf (Italian) parsley
2 teaspoons red wine vinegar
1 teaspoon lemon juice
¼ teaspoon sweet paprika
salt and pepper, to taste

to serve
sour cream
6 cooked prawns (shrimp), peeled,
  deveined and chopped, optional
chopped flat-leaf (Italian) parsley

method
1 Place all ingredients in a blender and puree until just smooth. Refrigerate until well chilled. Serve with a dollop of sour cream, some chopped prawns and a sprinkle of parsley.

Serves 4

Asparagus soup

To keep the lovely bright colour of this soup, discard the carrot before blending.

ingredients

20 g (³⁄₄ oz) butter

1 leek, white part only, washed well
  and sliced

¼ teaspoon crushed garlic

1 parsnip or small all-purpose potato,
  peeled and chopped

1 carrot, peeled and cut into
  large chunks

750 ml (26 fl oz/3 cups) chicken
  stock❖

500 g (1 lb 12 oz) fresh asparagus,
  woody ends cut off, stalks chopped

2 tablespoons plain Greek style yoghurt

½ teaspoon lemon juice

pinch freshly grated nutmeg

salt and pepper, to taste

to serve

snipped chives

method

1 In a large saucepan melt the butter then add the leek
and garlic and cook until the leek is soft. Add the parsnip
or potato, carrot and stock, bring to the boil then reduce
the heat and simmer for 5 minutes. Add the asparagus
and simmer for another 5 minutes or until the vegetables
are soft.

2 Allow the soup to cool a little then remove the carrot
and puree the rest, in batches, in a blender. You may
need to strain the soup at this stage if the asparagus
was a little stringy.

3 Blend in the yoghurt, lemon juice and nutmeg. Season to
taste with salt and pepper.

4 Sprinkle with snipped chives to serve.

Serves 4–6

Salsa soup

ingredients

750 ml (26 fl oz/3 cups) chicken stock❖
1 celery stalk, diced
1 small carrot, diced
200 g (7 oz) tinned corn kernels
200 g (7 oz) tinned black beans,
   drained and rinsed
185 g (6½ oz/¾ cup) commercial
   salsa❖, or to taste
175 g (6 oz/1 cup) chopped cooked
   chicken
1 tablespoon chopped coriander
   (cilantro) leaves

to serve

plain Greek style yoghurt
grated sharp cheese
chopped spring onions (scallions)
corn chips❖

method

1 Heat the stock to simmering point.
   Add the celery and carrot and
   simmer for a few minutes then add
   the drained corn and black beans.
   Stir in the salsa, using more or less to
   suit your taste. Add the chicken, heat
   through and stir in the coriander.
2 Serve the soup in bowls and top
   with a dollop of yoghurt, some
   cheese and spring onions. Serve
   with corn chips on the side.

Serves 4

Spiced sweet corn

method

The secrets to cooking really good corn are:

1 Always store fresh corn cobs at room temperature as refrigeration makes them starchy.
2 Bring a large saucepan of water to the boil and add 1 generous teaspoon of sugar — never salt.
3 Remove the husks and silk from the cobs, drop them into the boiling water and boil gently for 5 minutes. Don't be tempted to overcook them.
4 Serve the warm corn with lots of butter, fresh herbs and a sprinkle of ground salt. Try herbs such as thyme, parsley and oregano, or garlic. Lime juice, finely chopped chilli and chopped coriander (cilantro) leaves work well too.

Tortiche

You'll need to trim the tortillas as any excess that doesn't fit into the pie tins will become very dry and tough.

ingredients

4 corn tortillas❖

60 g (2¼ oz/½ cup) grated cheddar or other sharp cheese

155 g (5½ oz/¼ cup) finely diced red capsicum (pepper)

50 g (1¾ oz/¼ cup) tinned corn kernels

2 spring onions (scallions), chopped

2 eggs

2 egg yolks

125 g (4½ oz/½ cup) sour cream

60 ml (2 fl oz/¼ cup) milk

1 tablespoon chopped coriander (cilantro) leaves

½ teaspoon finely chopped mild chilli, optional

salt and pepper, to taste

method

1 Preheat oven to 180°C (350°F/Gas 4).

2 Grease four individual pie tins.

3 Warm tortillas briefly in the microwave until pliable. Gently press each one into a pie tin, trim away the overhang and place the tins onto a baking tray. Sprinkle the cheese, capsicum, corn and spring onions over the base of each tortilla.

4 In a bowl whisk together the eggs, egg yolks, sour cream, milk, coriander and chilli, if using. Season with salt and pepper.

5 Gently pour the egg mixture into the tortilla shells, filling them as much as you can. Don't worry if there are a few small leaks in the tortillas as they'll still cook just fine.

6 Place the baking tray into the oven and bake for 25–30 minutes until puffed and brown. Allow the tortiche to set in their tins for a few minutes then turn out onto a wire rack to cool.

7 Serve warm or at room temperature.

Makes 4

Corn and avocado salsa

ingredients

400 g (14 oz/2 cups) seeded and
  chopped roma (plum) tomatoes
200 g (7 oz/1 cup) tinned corn kernels
80 g (2¾ oz/½ cup) finely chopped
  yellow capsicum (pepper)
15 g (½ oz/¼ cup) finely chopped
  coriander (cilantro) leaves
1 tablespoon finely chopped red onion
1 red cayenne chilli, seeded and finely
  diced
¼ teaspoon salt
1 avocado, diced

dressing

2 tablespoons olive oil
1 tablespoon white wine vinegar
juice of 1 lime

method

1 Combine the dressing ingredients in a glass jar with
  a lid and shake well.
2 Combine all the salsa ingredients, except the avocado, in a
  bowl and mix well. Pour over the dressing and toss to coat,
  then add the avocado and toss gently.
3 Serve the salsa as a snack with corn chips❖, wrapped in
  a corn tortilla, or as part of a meal with fresh prawns
  (shrimp), grilled fish or chicken.

Tortillas or tacos with chilli beef

Corn tortillas make great wraps and are a good way to eat last night's leftovers, especially my favourite — shredded **Slow-roasted lamb** with **Quinoa tabouleh** and **Hummus**. Any filling you'd put on a sandwich can be used in a tortilla and you can even cook them in the sandwich maker, toasted-sandwich style. Make sure you buy corn tortillas and soften according to packet directions. In this recipe, soft or crisp tortillas can be used for the tacos.

ingredients

1 red onion, diced
1 tablespoon olive oil
500 g (1 lb 2 oz) lean minced (ground) beef
1 teaspoon crushed garlic
1 teaspoon ground cumin
1 teaspoon sweet paprika
¼ teaspoon cayenne pepper
400 g (14 oz) tin chopped tomatoes, with juice
300 g (10½ oz) tin kidney beans, drained and rinsed
125 ml (4 fl oz/½ cup) beef stock❖
salt and ground black pepper, to taste

to serve

8 corn tortillas or taco shells❖
shredded lettuce
shredded cheese
sour cream

method

1 In a large saucepan over low heat sauté the onion in the olive oil until softened. Increase the heat, add the beef and cook, stirring, until well browned, breaking up any lumps as you go. Add the garlic, cumin, paprika and cayenne pepper and stir until fragrant.

2 Stir in the tomatoes, kidney beans and stock, lower the heat and simmer, covered, for about 30 minutes, stirring occasionally, until thick. Season with salt and pepper.

3 Warm the tortillas or taco shells according to the packet directions, spoon in a little of the chilli beef and serve with shredded lettuce, shredded cheese, sour cream and **Corn and avocado salsa**.

Makes 8 tacos, serves 4

SOMETHING WITH A DRINK

Hummus

Once you've tried home-made hummus you won't go back to store-bought. It's quick and easy to make, is very versatile and keeps well in the refrigerator.

ingredients

400 g (14 oz) tin chickpeas, drained and rinsed

¼ teaspoon crushed garlic, or to taste

1 tablespoon tahini

2 tablespoons lemon juice

½ teaspoon sea salt

¼ teaspoon ground cumin

2 tablespoons olive oil

extra salt, to taste

method

1 In a food processor blend the chickpeas, garlic, tahini, lemon juice, sea salt and cumin. With the motor running, pour in the olive oil using only enough to make the mixture smooth — not too runny.

2 Spoon into a serving bowl and serve with rice crackers and vegetable sticks, or use as a spread on warm tortillas.

Beetroot hummus

Place 2 unpeeled beetroot (beets) into a large saucepan of boiling water, reduce the heat and simmer for 25–30 minutes until soft. Allow the beetroot to cool then rub off the skins and chop into chunks. Place into the blender with the chickpeas then proceed as above, using extra tahini or water to thin if necessary.

Smoked salmon pâté

ingredients

125 g (4½ oz) smoked salmon
60 g (2¼ oz) plain cream cheese, softened
1 tablespoon mayonnaise❖
1 tablespoon lemon juice
2 teaspoons chopped dill
1 teaspoon baby capers, rinsed

method

1 In the bowl of a food processor place the smoked salmon, cream cheese, mayonnaise, lemon juice and dill and blend until smooth. Stir through the capers, spoon into a serving bowl and chill overnight to firm up before serving.

2 Serve with gluten free crackers and wafers.

Guacamole

ingredients

4 ripe avocados

2 teaspoons lime juice

3 ripe roma (plum) tomatoes, seeded and diced

½ small red onion, finely diced

15 g (½ oz/¼ cup) finely chopped coriander (cilantro) leaves

¼ teaspoon crushed garlic, or to taste

1 red cayenne chilli, seeded and minced, or 1 teaspoon crushed chilli

salt and pepper, to taste

method

1 Mash the avocados with lime juice then add the rest of the ingredients and mix well.

2 To prevent the guacamole browning, place plastic wrap directly onto the surface, excluding any air, until ready to serve.

3 Serve the guacamole as a dip with corn chips✤ or vegetable sticks, or as part of a plate of nachos or tacos.

Satay sauce

Make this handy sauce at least a day ahead to give the flavours time to mellow — it can also be used as a marinade or dressing, thinned with water or extra coconut milk. If you're watching your salt intake, use unsalted peanuts but the taste won't be quite the same.

ingredients

160 g (5½ oz/1 cup) salted peanuts
1 tablespoon peanut oil
1 small onion, chopped
1 teaspoon crushed garlic
1 red chilli, seeded and chopped,
   or 1 teaspoon crushed chilli
1 tablespoon soft brown sugar
1 tablespoon soy sauce❖
1 tablespoon fish sauce❖
1 tablespoon lime juice (about 1 lime)
few drops sesame oil
salt, to taste
125–250 ml (4–9 fl oz/½–1 cup)
   coconut milk

method

1 In a hot dry frying pan roast the peanuts until they are golden brown, shaking the pan to keep the nuts moving and prevent burning.

2 In a separate pan heat the peanut oil and cook the onion and garlic until soft. Add the chilli, brown sugar and soy sauce and cook for another minute, stirring, until fragrant.

3 Place the mixture into the bowl of a food processor and puree until smooth. Add the peanuts, fish sauce, lime juice, sesame oil and salt and puree again. With the motor running, gradually add the coconut milk through the feed tube, using more or less, as needed, to give a good consistency.

4 Cover and store in the refrigerator. Before serving, warm gently and thin with a little extra coconut milk or water if necessary.

5 Serve with vegetable sticks or satays, or as a dressing on salads.

Makes 500 g (1 lb 2 oz/2 cups)

Taramasalata

ingredients

½ small red onion
100 g (3½ oz) jar red fish roe (tarama)
2 tablespoons lemon juice
2 tablespoons white wine vinegar
125 ml (4 fl oz/½ cup) olive oil
2 all-purpose potatoes (about 250 g/
   9 oz), steamed and finely mashed

method

1 In a food processor finely chop the onion then add the fish roe, lemon juice and vinegar and process. With the motor running, add the olive oil in a thin stream until combined.

2 Place the tarama mixture in a bowl and mix in the mashed potatoes until smooth. Don't be tempted to combine the potatoes in the food processor as they will become very gluey.

3 Cover and refrigerate for 24 hours to thicken up and for the flavours to develop.

4 Serve chilled with rice crackers or vegetable sticks.

Poppadoms with mint and cucumber raita

Allow three to four mini poppadoms per person, or more.

ingredients
250 g (9 oz/1 cup) plain Greek style
  yoghurt
1 Lebanese (short) cucumber, cut into
  small dice
¼ small red onion, finely diced
3 tablespoons finely chopped mint
¼ teaspoon ground cumin
¼ teaspoon salt
pinch sugar
pinch cayenne pepper

to serve
poppadoms

method
1 Lay out 4 poppadoms on a double
  layer of paper towel and spray
  lightly with cooking oil. Microwave
  on high for 40–60 seconds until
  puffed and crispy. Place on a wire
  rack to cool while cooking the
  remaining poppadoms.
2 Serve poppadoms warm or at room
  temperature with a bowl of **Mint
  and cucumber raita** for dipping.

MINT AND CUCUMBER RAITA
In a bowl combine the yoghurt with the
rest of the ingredients and mix well.

Spiced nuts

Almonds, raw cashews and macadamia nuts, pecans and peanuts all work well here.

ingredients
1 teaspoon ground salt
½ teaspoon ground chilli
½ teaspoon caster (superfine) sugar
¼ teaspoon Chinese five-spice
280 g (10 oz/2 cups) nuts of your choice

method
1 Preheat oven to 180°C (350°F/ Gas 4).
2 Combine the salt, chilli, sugar and five-spice in a bowl and mix well. Place the nuts onto a baking tray and spray very lightly with cooking oil. Sprinkle with the spice mix and roast in the oven for 5 minutes until golden, stirring to prevent burning. Serve warm from the oven. Store any leftover spice mix in the pantry.

Makes 280 g (10 oz/2 cups)

Spiced popcorn
In a large saucepan with a lid, heat 2 tablespoons vegetable oil over medium heat. Add 80 g (2¾ oz/⅓ cup) popping corn then cover and cook, shaking the pan until the popping subsides. Tip popcorn into a large serving bowl, sprinkle with spice mix and toss well to combine. Serve warm.

Thai style chicken balls

ingredients

90 g (3¼ oz/1 bunch) coriander (cilantro),
  leaves only, washed and dried
1 makrut (kaffir lime) leaf, centre vein
  removed
2½ tablespoons coconut cream
2 tablespoons fish sauce❖
1 tablespoon lime juice
1 tablespoon red curry paste❖
1 teaspoon crushed garlic
500 g (1 lb 2 oz) minced (ground)
  chicken
1 carrot, finely grated

dipping sauce

2 tablespoons water
1 tablespoon fish sauce❖
1 tablespoon lime juice
1 tablespoon roasted peanuts,
  finely chopped
1 tablespoon chopped coriander
  (cilantro) leaves
1 red cayenne chilli, finely chopped
2 teaspoons sugar
1 teaspoon cider vinegar

method

1 Preheat oven to 190°C (375°F/Gas 5).
2 Grease two 12-hole mini muffin tins.
3 In a food processor blend the coriander leaves, makrut
   leaf, coconut cream, fish sauce, lime juice, curry paste
   and garlic until the coriander is finely chopped. Pour into
   a large mixing bowl, add the chicken and grated carrot
   and mix well.
4 Spoon the mixture into the tins, filling to the top
   of each hole. Bake for 15–20 minutes until well browned,
   then turn out on a wire rack to cool a little. Repeat with
   the remaining mixture.
5 To serve, place the warm chicken balls with toothpicks
   onto a serving plate, with a bowl of **Dipping sauce**
   alongside.

Makes about 3 dozen

DIPPING SAUCE

In a bowl mix all ingredients together and stir to dissolve the
sugar. Serve at room temperature.

Prawns and asparagus with lemon and dill mayonnaise

ingredients

2 egg yolks

2 tablespoons lemon juice

250 ml (9 fl oz/1 cup) macadamia oil
   or mild olive oil

1 tablespoon finely chopped dill

salt and pepper or pinch of sugar,
   to taste

350 g (12 oz/2 bunches) asparagus

500 g (1 lb 2 oz) cooked prawns
   (shrimp)

method

1 To make the mayonnaise, place egg yolks and lemon juice into a food processor and process until well combined. With the motor running, add the oil in a thin stream and process until thick. Stir through the dill then season to taste.

2 Choose a pan large enough to hold the asparagus flat, half-fill with water and bring to the boil. Trim the woody ends from the asparagus and place in the boiling water. When the water returns to the boil, drain the asparagus and cool immediately in iced water.

3 Serve asparagus at room temperature with cold prawns and a bowl of mayonnaise for dipping.

Basil mayonnaise
Substitute the dill with 1 tablespoon chopped basil.

Cheddar shortbread

These biscuits are best eaten warm from the oven but the dough can be prepared ahead and refrigerated until needed.

ingredients

110 g (3¾ oz/1 cup) commercial gluten free plain (all-purpose) flour✤, measured after sifting
¾ teaspoon salt
¼ teaspoon cayenne pepper, or to taste
40 g (1½ oz) butter, chopped
60 g (2¼ oz/½ cup) grated cheddar cheese
1 tablespoon finely chopped chives
60 ml (2 fl oz/¼ cup) milk

method

1 Preheat oven to 180°C (350°F/Gas 4).
2 Line a baking tray with baking paper.
3 Place the flour, salt and cayenne pepper in a food processor and pulse to mix. Add the butter and process until the mixture looks like breadcrumbs then add the cheese and chives and process until combined. With the motor running, pour the milk in through the feed tube, using only enough milk for the mixture to form a ball.
4 Remove the dough, place onto a sheet of baking paper and use the paper to roll and form the dough into a long log shape. Leave wrapped in the paper, wrap tightly again with plastic wrap and refrigerate for at least 1 hour.
5 Remove the wrapping and cut the log into 5 mm (¼ in) disks. Place onto the baking tray and bake for 15–20 minutes until lightly browned, turning the biscuits over after 10 minutes. Cool on a wire rack.

Makes about 18

Mini quiches with red onion marmalade

ingredients

5 eggs
250 g (9 oz/1 cup) fresh ricotta cheese
1½ tablespoons cream
35 g (1¼ oz/¼ cup) grated gruyère
   cheese
2 tablespoons white rice flour
2 tablespoons chopped chives
½ teaspoon salt
pepper, to taste

red onion marmalade

1 tablespoon olive oil
30 g (1 oz) butter
3 red onions, finely sliced
2 tablespoons balsamic vinegar
1 tablespoon soft brown sugar

method

1 Preheat oven to 180°C (350°F/Gas 4).
2 Grease two 12-hole mini muffin tins.
3 Whisk the eggs, ricotta cheese and cream in a bowl until combined. Add the cheese, rice flour, chives and salt and pepper and mix well.
4 Pour dessertspoons of the mixture into the muffin tins and bake for 15–20 minutes or until brown and puffed.
5 Remove the quiches from the tins and repeat with the remaining mixture.
6 Serve the quiches warm or at room temperature, topped with some **Red onion marmalade**.

Makes about 30

RED ONION MARMALADE

Heat the olive oil and butter in a heavy-based saucepan then add the onions and vinegar. Cook, covered, over low heat until very soft, about 20 minutes. Add the brown sugar and cook, uncovered, for a few more minutes until caramelized. Serve at room temperature.

Smoked salmon and leek frittata

This makes a party-sized frittata — for a smaller gathering, simply halve the quantities.

ingredients

1 tablespoon olive oil
2 leeks, white part only, washed and
    finely sliced
3 large all-purpose potatoes, peeled, cut
    into 5 mm ($\frac{1}{4}$ in) slices and steamed
    until soft
100 g ($3\frac{1}{2}$ oz) smoked salmon, chopped
    into 2 cm ($\frac{3}{4}$ in) pieces
12 large eggs
60 g ($2\frac{1}{4}$ oz/$\frac{1}{4}$ cup) sour cream
65 g ($2\frac{1}{4}$ oz/$\frac{1}{2}$ cup) grated gruyère
    cheese
1 tablespoon chopped dill
salt and ground black pepper, to taste

method

1 Preheat oven to 180°C (350°F/Gas 4).
2 Grease a 5 cm (2 in) deep, 33 x 23 cm (13 x 9 in)
    baking tin.
3 Heat the olive oil in a frying pan and cook the leeks until
    soft. Place into the prepared baking tin and top with the
    potato slices and salmon.
4 Mix together the eggs, sour cream, cheese and dill.
    Season with salt and plenty of ground black pepper. Pour
    the egg mixture evenly over the potato and salmon.
5 Bake for 35–40 minutes until puffed and golden. Serve at
    room temperature, cut into 4 cm ($1\frac{1}{2}$ in) squares.

Makes about 40 pieces

Baked polenta

This is a really versatile dish to have in the refrigerator as it can be served under eggs, baked beans or ratatouille, or with any dish with lots of sauce. It can also be used for dips — cut the baked polenta into sticks, roll in extra parmesan and fry in a little olive oil.

ingredients

500 ml (17 fl oz/2 cups) chicken stock❖
500 ml (17 fl oz/2 cups) water
175 g (6 oz/1 cup) polenta
1 teaspoon salt
¼ teaspoon ground black pepper
3 tablespoons chopped flat-leaf (Italian) parsley
2 tablespoons plain Greek style yoghurt
25 g (1 oz/¼ cup) grated parmesan cheese

variations

For variations on plain polenta try adding:
❖ caramelized onion
❖ 1 teaspoon dried rosemary or dried sage
❖ 30 g (1 oz/¼ cup) diced prosciutto and 1 teaspoon dried thyme
❖ 2 leeks, sautéed, and 40 g (1½ oz/ ¼ cup) toasted pine nuts

method

1 Preheat oven to 180°C (350°F/Gas 4).
2 Grease a 21 cm (8¼ in) square baking tin.
3 Pour the stock and water into the baking tin and whisk in the polenta and salt and pepper. Bake, uncovered, for 30 minutes. Mix together the parsley, yoghurt and parmesan.
4 Remove the polenta from the oven and stir lightly then add the yoghurt mixture and stir to blend. Return to the oven and continue to bake, uncovered, until all the liquid has absorbed, about another 10 minutes.
5 At this stage the polenta can be served as it is, in a creamy consistency, but I prefer to make this dish ahead and let it firm up overnight, covered, in the refrigerator. The next day turn out the polenta onto a chopping board and cut into triangles or squares. Grill (broil) or fry in a little olive oil until golden and serve.

Serves 6 as part of a meal

Ratatouille

Make this at least a day ahead and serve hot or at room temperature. If you prefer your ratatouille more on the mushy side, let the vegetables simmer for an extra ten minutes. Serve with **Baked polenta** or mashed sweet potato with pumpkin.

ingredients

1 large onion, finely sliced
2 tablespoons olive oil
1 teaspoon crushed garlic
1 large eggplant (aubergine), about
   500 g (1 lb 2 oz), chopped
¼ teaspoon ground coriander
2 zucchini (courgettes), chopped
1 small red capsicum (pepper), seeded
   and diced
1 small yellow capsicum (pepper),
   seeded and diced
2 yellow baby (pattypan) squash,
   chopped
1 kg (2 lb 4 oz) ripe roma (plum)
   tomatoes, peeled and chopped
125 ml (4 fl oz/½ cup) white wine
1 tablespoon tomato paste
   (concentrated puree)
3 thyme sprigs
1 bay leaf
2 tablespoons chopped basil
1 tablespoon chopped flat-leaf (Italian)
   parsley
1 teaspoon salt
good grind of black pepper

method

1 In a large saucepan over medium heat sauté the onion in olive oil until soft. Add the garlic, eggplant and coriander and cook, stirring, for 5 minutes. Add the zucchini, red and yellow capsicums and squash and cook for another few minutes.

2 Stir in the tomatoes, wine, tomato paste, thyme and bay leaf, lower the heat and simmer, covered, for about 15 minutes until vegetables are tender. Stir in the basil and parsley and season to taste with salt and pepper.

Serves 6 as a side dish

Panzanella

ingredients

1 tablespoon balsamic vinegar

2½ tablespoons olive oil

100 g (3½ oz) tinned cannellini beans,
   drained and rinsed

2 roma (plum) tomatoes, chopped

1 Lebanese (short) cucumber, chopped

½ small red onion, finely diced

1 tablespoon baby capers, rinsed

100 g (3½ oz/¾ cup) pitted black olives

1 tablespoon shredded basil

method

1 In a glass jar with a lid combine the balsamic vinegar with the olive oil and shake well. In a serving bowl combine the rest of the ingredients, mix well then pour over the dressing and toss to coat evenly.

2 Serve with grilled fish or chicken, with some home-made **Basil mayonnaise** and mashed potatoes on the side.

Serves 6 as a side dish

Pork and pistachio terrine

What would a picnic be without a terrine?

ingredients

12 slices prosciutto

1 kg (2 lb 4 oz) minced (ground) pork
and veal

80 g (2¾ oz/½ cup) pistachio nuts,
skinned

1 small red onion, finely chopped

1 green apple, grated

10 g (¼ oz/¼ cup) chopped sage leaves

1 tablespoon chopped flat-leaf (Italian)
parsley

2 eggs, lightly beaten

2 teaspoons pink peppercorns

1 teaspoon sea salt

½ teaspoon ground black pepper

method

1 Preheat the oven to 170°C (325°F/Gas 3).
2 Prepare a water bath and grease a terrine mould or
large loaf tin.
3 Line the terrine mould with the prosciutto slices, allowing
the ends to overhang the sides of the mould.
4 Combine the rest of the ingredients in a large bowl and,
using your hands, mix well. Pack the meat mixture into
the mould, pressing firmly to remove any air pockets, then
fold over the prosciutto. Cover the terrine with a lid or foil
and place in the water bath.
5 Bake for 90 minutes or until the cooking juices run clear.
6 Drain off the excess liquid and skim the surface then allow
the terrine to cool in the mould. When cold, remove from
the mould and wrap the terrine securely in foil. Refrigerate
for 24 hours to allow the flavours to develop.
7 Serve with **Quince and cranberry chutney**, a good
strong cheddar cheese and **French potato salad**.

Quince and cranberry chutney

In a saucepan sweat 1 small diced red capsicum (pepper), 1 small diced red onion, ½ teaspoon ground
coriander and ½ teaspoon mustard seeds in a little oil until softened. Add 120 g (4¼ oz/1 cup) dried
cranberries, 50 g (1¾ oz) chopped quince paste, 55 g (2 oz/¼ cup) soft brown sugar, 75 g (2½ oz/½ cup)
currants, ½ teaspoon chilli flakes, 1 teaspoon salt, 60 ml (2 fl oz/¼ cup) cider vinegar, 60 ml (2 fl oz/¼ cup)
apple juice and 1 strip of lemon zest. Stir over low heat until the quince paste is dissolved then simmer,
covered, for 30 minutes, stirring occasionally. Thin with more apple juice if necessary, bearing in mind that
it will firm up some more once chilled. Store, covered, in the refrigerator for at least 24 hours before
serving, but this will keep maturing for about a week.

Vietnamese rice paper rolls

There is a definite art to rolling these without splitting the rice paper but practice makes perfect. My best tips are don't oversoak the rice paper sheets and don't overfill them.

ingredients

12 round or square dried rice paper
  sheets
100 g (3½ oz) rice vermicelli, soaked in
  hot water until soft, drained
500 g (1 lb 2 oz) cooked prawns
  (shrimp), peeled, deveined and finely
  chopped
1 carrot, cut into fine matchsticks
½ yellow capsicum (pepper), cut into fine
  matchsticks
45 g (1½ oz/½ cup) mung bean or
  snow pea sprouts
2 red cayenne chillies, seeded and
  finely diced
1 tablespoon chopped coriander
  (cilantro) leaves
1 tablespoon chopped Vietnamese mint
  or regular mint

dipping sauce

2 tablespoons water
1 tablespoon fish sauce❖
1 tablespoon lime juice
1 tablespoon roasted peanuts, chopped
1 tablespoon chopped coriander
  (cilantro) leaves
1 red cayenne chilli, finely chopped
2 teaspoons sugar
1 teaspoon cider vinegar

method

1 Soak the rice paper sheets in warm water, one at a time, until just soft then drain on a clean tea towel (dish towel).
2 Place a small amount of each of the filling ingredients in a little pile along the rice paper, sprinkle with some herbs and roll up, tucking in the sides as you go. Repeat with the remaining rice paper sheets and ingredients and serve at room temperature with the **Dipping sauce**.

Makes 12

DIPPING SAUCE

Mix all ingredients together in a bowl and stir to dissolve the sugar. Serve at room temperature.

Soy and honey-glazed chicken

ingredients

12 chicken drumsticks with skin
1 tablespoon honey
1 tablespoon olive oil
1 tablespoon soy sauce❖
1½ teaspoons Chinese five-spice
1 teaspoon crushed garlic

method

1 Place the drumsticks into a glass or stainless steel bowl.
2 Heat the honey in the microwave until very runny then add the olive oil, soy sauce, five-spice and garlic. Stir well to combine, then pour over the drumsticks and mix to coat. Allow the pieces to marinate for a few hours then bake in a 180°C (350°F/Gas 4) oven for 45–50 minutes or until cooked through, turning and brushing with the glaze a few times.
3 When the chicken legs are cooked, place onto a large platter and serve with a generous bowl of **Tahini coleslaw** and some fresh cobs of **Spiced sweet corn**.

Serves 4–6

Baked omelette with spinach and caramelized onion

ingredients

30 g (1 oz) butter
2 red onions, finely sliced
1 teaspoon ground coriander
2 teaspoons soft brown sugar
350 g (12 oz/1 bunch) English spinach, washed well and roughly chopped
250 g (9 oz/1 cup) fresh ricotta cheese
50 g ($1^{3}/_{4}$ oz/$^{1}/_{2}$ cup) finely grated parmesan cheese
35 g ($1^{1}/_{4}$ oz/$^{1}/_{4}$ cup) finely grated gruyère cheese
9 eggs
35 g ($1^{1}/_{4}$ oz/$^{1}/_{4}$ cup) **Rice flour blend**
1 teaspoon salt

method

1 Preheat oven to 180°C (350°F/Gas 4).
2 Grease and line a large 24 cm ($9^{1}/_{2}$ in) spring-form tin.
3 In a frying pan melt the butter and cook the onions and coriander until the onions are soft. Stir in the sugar, reduce the heat and cook, covered, until the onions are caramelized, stirring occasionally. Allow to cool.
4 Steam the chopped spinach until just wilted then squeeze out the excess moisture.
5 In a food processor blend the ricotta, parmesan and gruyère cheeses with the eggs until smooth. Add the flour and salt, blend again then place the mixture into a large bowl.
6 Stir through the caramelized onion and spinach, mix well and pour into the prepared tin. Bake for about 45 minutes until puffed and evenly browned.
7 Remove from the oven and allow to firm up in the tin for a few minutes — the omelette will sink back while cooling.
8 Turn out onto a plate and remove the baking paper then invert onto a serving plate. Serve warm or at room temperature.

Serves 6

Curried sweet potato cakes with raita

ingredients

500 g (1 lb 2 oz) orange sweet potato,
   peeled and chopped
150 g (5½ oz) waxy potatoes, peeled
   and chopped
200 g (7 oz/1⅓ cups) tinned chickpeas,
   drained and rinsed
1 tablespoon tahini
1 tablespoon lemon juice
1 generous tablespoon curry paste❖
15 g (½ oz/¼ cup) chopped coriander
   (cilantro) leaves
1 egg
½ teaspoon salt, or to taste
besan (chickpea flour) or rice flour,
   for coating
canola oil

method

1 Steam the sweet potato and potato until soft then mash
   with a food mill or ricer.
2 Place the chickpeas, tahini, lemon juice, curry paste,
   coriander, egg and salt into a food processor and blend
   until smooth. Add to the mashed potatoes and mix
   well to combine.
3 To make the mixture easier to handle, place it in the
   refrigerator, uncovered, for 1 hour to dry out a little.
4 Form the mixture into patties, roll lightly in the flour
   and fry in a little hot oil until browned on both sides.
5 Serve warm, drizzled generously with **Mint and
   cucumber raita**.

Makes about 16 patties

Thai beef salad

ingredients

50 g (1¾ oz) rice vermicelli
500 g (1 lb 2 oz) sirloin steak
sesame oil
1 whole makrut (kaffir lime) leaf, middle
   vein discarded, and finely chopped
15 g (½ oz/¼ cup) finely chopped
   Vietnamese mint
20 g (¾ oz/⅓ cup) finely chopped
   coriander (cilantro) leaves
½ small red onion, thinly sliced
1 Lebanese (short) cucumber, peeled,
   cut into matchsticks
1 carrot, cut into matchsticks
50 g (1¾ oz) snow peas (mangetout),
   cut into matchsticks
¼ small red capsicum (pepper),
   finely diced
¼ small Chinese cabbage, shredded
1 small handful bean sprouts
2 spring onions (scallions), finely
   chopped
40 g (1½ oz/¼ cup) unsalted, roasted
   peanuts, chopped

dressing

80 ml (2½ fl oz/⅓ cup) peanut oil
2 tablespoons fish sauce❖
1 teaspoon crushed chilli
juice of 1 lime
2 teaspoons caster (superfine) sugar

method

1 Soak vermicelli noodles in warm water for a few minutes
   until soft then drain and chop into shorter lengths.
2 Brush the steak with sesame oil and chargrill or pan-fry
   over high heat until cooked to your liking. Rest steak for
   10 minutes then slice thinly.
3 Combine the sliced beef with the remaining ingredients
   and mix together well.
4 Combine all the dressing ingredients, stirring to dissolve
   the sugar. Pour the dressing over the salad, toss to coat
   and serve at room temperature.

Serves 4

This dish is also delicious using prawns (shrimp) or chicken
instead of beef.

Vegetable pilaf with chicken and feta salad

ingredients

1 double boneless, skinless chicken
  breast
200 g (7 oz) peeled pumpkin (winter
  squash)
2 tablespoons olive oil
1 small onion, sliced
½ teaspoon ground cumin
200 g (7 oz/1 cup) basmati rice
625 ml (21 fl oz/2½ cups) chicken
  stock❖
75 g (2½ oz/½ cup) tinned chickpeas,
  drained and rinsed
25 g (1 oz/½ cup) chopped coriander
  (cilantro) leaves
400 g (14 oz) tin artichoke hearts,
  drained and quartered
35 g (1¼ oz/1 cup) baby rocket (arugula)
1 small red onion, finely chopped
80 g (2¾ oz/½ cup) pine nuts, toasted
1 tablespoon currants
200 g (7 oz) feta cheese, crumbled

dressing

125 ml (4 fl oz/½ cup) olive oil, extra
juice of ½ lemon
salt, to taste

method

1 Poach the chicken fillet, cool and cut into bite- sized
   pieces.
2 Roast the pumpkin in a 180°C (350°F/Gas 4) oven until
   soft. Chop the pumpkin into small dice.
3 Place the olive oil, onion and cumin in a saucepan and
   cook over low heat until the onion is very soft. Add the rice
   and stock to the pan, cover and bring to the boil then
   reduce the heat and simmer until the rice is cooked. Stir
   through the chickpeas and coriander then gently add the
   pumpkin. Cover and keep warm until ready to serve.
4 Combine the chicken, artichokes, rocket, red onion, pine
   nuts and currants in a large bowl.
5 Combine the dressing ingredients and pour over the
   salad. Toss to coat with the dressing.
6 To serve, place the warm pilaf onto a serving plate,
   top with the chicken salad and sprinkle with crumbled
   feta cheese.

Serves 4

Pesto lamb with sweet potato salad

Following the motto 'if they sell it in shops I don't make it', a good commercially prepared pesto❖ can be substituted here.

ingredients

2 lamb backstrap or loin fillets, about
   500 g (1 lb 2 oz)
600 g (1 lb 5 oz) orange sweet potato,
   peeled, sliced and roasted
100 g (3½ oz) baby English spinach,
   washed and dried
100 g (3½ oz) rocket (arugula), washed
   and dried
250 g (9 oz) cherry tomatoes, halved
½ small red onion, finely diced
80 g (2¾ oz/½ cup) pine nuts, toasted
2 tablespoons balsamic vinegar
3 tablespoons olive oil
125 g (4½ oz/½ cup) **Basil pesto**
7 g (¼ oz/¼ cup) finely chopped parsley

method

1 Barbecue or grill (broil) the lamb until medium or to your taste. When cooked, wrap in foil and cool.
2 Chop the roasted sweet potato slices into quarters and mix with the spinach, rocket, tomatoes, onion and pine nuts. Whisk together the balsamic vinegar and olive oil, then pour over the salad ingredients and toss to coat. Place the salad onto a serving plate.
3 In a bowl mix the pesto and parsley together. Slice the lamb fillet on the diagonal, toss in the pesto until well coated then place on top of the sweet potato salad.

Serves 4

BASIL PESTO

Place 100 g (3½ oz/2 cups) basil leaves, 40 g (1½ oz/¼ cup) toasted pine nuts, 25 g (1 oz/¼ cup) grated parmesan cheese and 1 teaspoon crushed garlic into the bowl of a food processor and process to combine. With the motor running, add 60 ml (2 fl oz/¼ cup) olive oil in a steady stream and puree. Season to taste with salt and pepper and thin with a little water if you prefer.

Makes about 250 g (9 oz/1 cup)

Steamed mussels with white wine, garlic and chilli

ingredients

2 kg (4 lb 8 oz) mussels
2 tablespoons olive oil
2 tablespoons butter
2 teaspoons crushed garlic
1 teaspoon crushed chilli
125 ml (4 fl oz/½ cup) white wine
250 ml (9 fl oz/1 cup) water
15 g (½ oz/½ cup) chopped flat-leaf
  (Italian) parsley

to serve

370 g (13 oz/2 cups) cooked
  jasmine rice

method

1 Scrub the mussels under running water, removing the beards and discarding any that are opened or have broken shells.
2 In a large saucepan or a wok with a lid place the olive oil, butter, garlic, chilli, white wine and water. Bring to the boil then add the mussels and stir to coat with the broth. Cover with the lid. Steam the mussels over medium heat for 5 minutes, then remove any that have opened to a large serving bowl. Replace the lid and steam the remaining mussels for another 2 minutes, discarding any that haven't opened inside 8 minutes. Place the rest of the mussels into the serving bowl, pour over the wine broth and toss through the parsley.
3 To serve, place a spoonful of rice into large individual bowls, pile some mussels on top and spoon over a little broth. Place the rest of the mussels and extra rice in the centre of the table for second helpings.

Serves 4

Jambalaya

ingredients

olive oil

250 g (9 oz) boneless, skinless chicken breast, chopped

1 onion, diced

70 g (2½ oz/½ cup) chopped celery

40 g (1½ oz/¼ cup) chopped red capsicum (pepper)

40 g (1½ oz/¼ cup) chopped yellow capsicum (pepper)

80 g (2¾ oz/½ cup) diced ham

1 teaspoon crushed garlic

2 tablespoons tomato paste (concentrated puree)

2 teaspoons thyme leaves

½ teaspoon sugar, or to taste

200 g (7 oz/1 cup) long-grain rice

½ teaspoon sweet Hungarian paprika

1 red cayenne chilli, seeded and finely chopped

400 g (14 oz) tin peeled, diced tomatoes, drained

375 ml (13 fl oz/1½ cups) chicken stock❖

250 ml (9 fl oz/1 cup) dry white wine

400 g (14 oz) raw prawns (shrimp), peeled, deveined and halved

7 g (¼ oz/¼ cup) chopped flat-leaf (Italian) parsley

2 spring onions (scallions), diced

salt and pepper, to taste

method

1 Heat the olive oil in a large deep frying pan and brown the chicken over high heat. Remove the chicken to a bowl, reduce the heat and add the onion to the pan. Sauté until softened then add the celery, red and yellow capsicums, ham and garlic and stir for a few more minutes. Stir in the tomato paste, thyme and sugar and mix well.

2 Add the rice, paprika, chilli, tomatoes, stock and white wine, stir to combine and bring to the boil. Reduce the heat and simmer, covered, for 15–20 minutes until the rice is almost cooked. Add the prawns and cook for another 5 minutes or until the prawns are pink and cooked.

3 Return the chicken to the pan and heat through, mix in the parsley and spring onions and season with salt and pepper.

Serves 4

Fresh rice noodles with chicken and coriander pesto

ingredients

2 boneless, skinless chicken breasts, poached and shredded

600 g (1 lb 5 oz) fresh rice noodles❖

1 Lebanese (short) cucumber, chopped

2 roma (plum) tomatoes, seeded and chopped, or 12 grape tomatoes, halved

coriander pesto

60 g (2¼ oz/⅓ cup) unsalted peanuts

60 g (2¼ oz/⅓ cup) macadamia nuts

1 teaspoon crushed ginger

1 teaspoon crushed garlic

½ teaspoon crushed chilli, or to taste

30 g (1 oz/1 cup) coriander (cilantro) leaves

5 g (⅛ oz/¼ cup) Vietnamese mint or regular mint

15 g (½ oz/¼ cup) basil leaves

2 spring onions (scallions)

150 ml (5 fl oz) peanut oil

1 tablespoon macadamia oil

2 tablespoons lime juice

1 teaspoon fish sauce❖

salt, to taste

method

1 To make the coriander pesto, toast the peanuts and macadamia nuts in a hot dry frying pan until lightly browned. Combine the cooled nuts, ginger, garlic and chilli in a food processor and process to form a paste. Add the herbs and process until finely chopped. With the motor running, add the peanut oil and macadamia oil in a steady stream. Add the lime juice and fish sauce and blend until combined. Transfer the pesto to a bowl, press plastic wrap onto the surface to exclude any air, cover and refrigerate until needed.

2 Put the chicken in a large saucepan, add the pesto and toss to combine and gently warm over low heat. Heat the rice noodles in the microwave or following the packet directions. Add the noodles to the pan and toss gently to combine with the pesto and chicken.

3 To serve, place warm pesto noodles into bowls and top with the cucumber and tomatoes.

Serves 4

San choy bau

ingredients

1 onion, diced
2 tablespoons peanut oil
500 g (1 lb 2 oz) minced (ground) pork
1 teaspoon crushed garlic
50 g (1¾ oz/½ cup) chopped button
   mushrooms
2 teaspoons sugar
2 teaspoons fish sauce❖
1 tablespoon cider vinegar
1 teaspoon crushed chilli
1 large carrot, grated
15 g (½ oz/¼ cup) combined chopped
   Vietnamese mint and coriander
   (cilantro) leaves
3 spring onions (scallions), chopped
40 g (1½ oz/¼ cup) roasted peanuts,
   chopped
45 g (1½ oz/½ cup) bean sprouts
salt, to taste

to serve

iceberg lettuce leaves, cooked rice,
   chopped Vietnamese mint

dipping sauce

2 tablespoons water
1 tablespoon fish sauce❖
1 tablespoon lime juice
1 tablespoon roasted peanuts, finely
   chopped
1 tablespoon chopped coriander
   (cilantro) leaves
1 red cayenne chilli, finely chopped
2 teaspoons sugar
1 teaspoon cider vinegar

method

1 Cook the onion in peanut oil over medium heat until soft
   then increase the heat and add the pork and garlic. Stir-
   fry until the meat browns then add the mushrooms, sugar,
   fish sauce, vinegar and chilli. Mix together and cook for
   1–2 minutes then add the grated carrot, herbs and spring
   onions and toss through.

2 Just before serving, add the chopped peanuts and bean
   sprouts.

3 To serve, place a lettuce cup into a bowl, add a little rice
   and a spoonful of pork and sprinkle with chopped
   Vietnamese mint. Roll up and eat with your fingers with a
   small bowl of **Dipping sauce** on the side.

Serves 4

DIPPING SAUCE

In a bowl mix all ingredients together and stir to dissolve the
sugar. Serve at room temperature.

Poached salmon with hollandaise sauce

250 ml (9 fl oz/1 cup) white wine
250 ml (9 fl oz/1 cup) water
few dill sprigs
1 teaspoon black peppercorns
zest of 1 lemon
4 salmon fillets

hollandaise sauce
3 egg yolks
1 tablespoon lemon juice
125 g (4½ oz) butter, cut into small
    pieces

method
1 In a large frying pan bring the wine and water to a gentle simmer. Add the dill, peppercorns, lemon zest and salmon fillets. Cover and poach the salmon gently over low heat for 5–7 minutes, depending on the thickness of the fillets.
2 Place a salmon fillet onto a warmed serving plate and spoon over a little **Hollandaise sauce**. Serve with boiled new potatoes and steamed sugar snap peas.

Serves 4

HOLLANDAISE SAUCE
In the top of a double boiler over gently simmering water, combine the egg yolks, 1 tablespoon water and lemon juice and whisk until the mixture starts to thicken. Add the butter one piece at a time, whisking constantly until the sauce is thick and creamy.

Chicken souvlaki with tzatziki

ingredients

3 tablespoons olive oil
2 tablespoons white wine vinegar
1 tablespoon lemon juice
½ small red onion, diced
1 teaspoon dried oregano
2 double boneless, skinless chicken
   breasts, cut into large cubes
skewers soaked in water

tzatziki

1 Lebanese (short) cucumber
250 g (9 oz/1 cup) plain Greek style
   yoghurt
1 teaspoon crushed garlic
1 teaspoon white wine vinegar
1 teaspoon chopped dill
½ teaspoon salt

method

1   In a glass or stainless steel bowl combine the olive oil, vinegar, lemon juice, onion and oregano. Add the chicken and stir to coat then cover and marinate in the refrigerator for a few hours or overnight.
2   Remove the chicken pieces from the marinade and thread onto skewers. Barbecue or grill (broil) until cooked through, turning to brown evenly.
3   Serve chicken souvlaki with **Tzatziki** and a **Greek salad**.

Serves 4

TZATZIKI

Grate the cucumber and squeeze out the excess moisture. In a bowl combine the grated cucumber, yoghurt, garlic, vinegar, dill and salt and mix well.

Turkey, green bean and mushroom stir-fry

ingredients

1 tablespoon peanut oil
1 onion, peeled and sliced into thin
  wedges
½ teaspoon crushed garlic
1 teaspoon grated fresh ginger
500 g (1 lb 2 oz) minced (ground) turkey
1 small yellow capsicum (pepper), diced
150 g (5½ oz) button mushrooms,
  chopped
250 ml (9 fl oz/1 cup) chicken stock❖
1 tablespoon oyster sauce❖
1 tablespoon fish sauce❖
125 g (4½ oz) snake (yard-long) beans
  or green beans, chopped
¼ small Chinese cabbage, shredded
1 tablespoon chopped coriander
  (cilantro) leaves
1 handful bean sprouts, rinsed
sesame oil

to serve

185 g (6½ oz/1 cup) cooked rice
chopped coriander (cilantro) leaves,
  extra

method

1 Heat the peanut oil in a wok and cook the onion, garlic and ginger until the onion is softened. Add the turkey, capsicum and mushrooms and stir-fry until browned. Add the stock, oyster sauce and fish sauce. Reduce the heat and simmer, covered, for about 5 minutes then add the beans and cook for another 5 minutes.

2 Add the cabbage and coriander to the wok and cook briefly. Just before serving, stir through the bean sprouts and a few drops of sesame oil.

3 To serve, spoon rice into individual serving bowls, top with the stir-fry and sprinkle with extra chopped coriander.

Serves 4

Sunday spiced pilaf

Any combination of leftover meat and vegetables can be used in this end-of-the-week tidy-up.

ingredients

1 onion, diced
1 tablespoon olive oil
200 g (7 oz/1 cup) basmati rice
500 ml (17 fl oz/2 cups) stock❖
pinch salt
1 tablespoon olive oil, extra
2 teaspoons ground coriander
1 teaspoon crushed chilli
1 teaspoon crushed garlic
½ yellow capsicum (pepper), diced
1 carrot, chopped
1 handful green beans, chopped
350 g (12 oz/2 cups) leftover chopped
   lamb, chicken or beef
75 g (2½ oz/½ cup) tinned chickpeas,
   drained and rinsed
1 handful English spinach leaves,
   shredded
25 g (1 oz/½ cup) chopped coriander
   (cilantro) leaves
35 g (1¼ oz/¼ cup) pistachio nuts,
   chopped
salt and pepper, to taste

method

1 In a saucepan or rice maker sweat the onion in olive oil until soft then add the rice, stock and salt. Cook until all the liquid is absorbed, then fluff with a fork and leave, covered, for another 10 minutes.

2 In a wok heat the extra olive oil and fry the spices until fragrant. Add the capsicum, carrot and beans and stir-fry until softened. Add the meat, chickpeas and spinach and stir until heated through. Add the cooked rice, toss well to combine then add the coriander and pistachio nuts. Season with salt and pepper.

Serves 4

Grilled tuna with white bean puree

ingredients

600 g (1 lb 5 oz) fresh tuna or swordfish
   fillets
olive oil
juice of 1 lemon
1 lemon, quartered

white bean puree

2 x 400 g (14 oz) tins cannellini beans,
   rinsed and drained
1 teaspoon crushed garlic
60 ml (2 fl oz/¼ cup) lemon juice
olive oil
1 tablespoon chopped dill
1 tablespoon chopped parsley
2 tablespoons baby capers, rinsed

method

1 To make the white bean puree, combine the cannellini beans, garlic and lemon juice in a food processor. With the motor running, pour in enough olive oil to make a puree. Remove to an ovenproof dish and stir through the dill, parsley and baby capers. Cover and keep warm in a 180°C (350°F/Gas 4) oven for 15 minutes.

2 Brush the tuna or swordfish fillets with the combined olive oil and lemon juice. Barbecue the fish until cooked to your liking.

3 To serve, place a generous spoonful of white bean puree onto a serving plate and top with a piece of barbecued fish. Serve with lemon quarters for squeezing over the fish, and with a green salad with olives.

Serves 4

Tuna and white bean dip

Drain a 185 g (6½ oz) tin of tuna packed in oil. Add the tuna and beans to the food processor. Proceed as above but don't bother warming the dip in the oven. This dips keeps well, covered, in the refrigerator, and is great spread on rice crackers for a quick and filling snack.

Chicken cacciatore with eggplant

ingredients

2 large eggplants (aubergines), sliced
olive oil
1 kg (2 lb 4 oz) boneless, skinless
   thighs, chopped into bite-sized pieces
1 teaspoon crushed garlic
1 small yellow capsicum (pepper), diced
150 g (5½ oz) prosciutto, chopped
250 ml (9 fl oz/1 cup) white wine
400 g (14 oz) tin peeled, diced tomatoes
   with juice
1 tablespoon tomato paste
   (concentrated puree)

to serve

chopped flat-leaf (Italian) parsley
pitted black olives
grated parmesan cheese

method

1 Brush the eggplant slices with olive oil and grill (broil) until well browned. When cool, cut into smaller pieces.
2 Fry the chicken pieces in a little hot olive oil until brown then add the garlic, capsicum and prosciutto and cook briefly.
3 Add the wine, tomatoes and tomato paste, lower the heat and simmer, covered, for 20 minutes. Stir in the eggplant, cover and cook for another 10 minutes until the chicken is tender.
4 To serve, sprinkle with chopped parsley, a few pitted and sliced black olives and grated parmesan cheese. Serve with sweet potato and pumpkin (winter squash) mash and some lightly steamed carrots on the side.

Serves 4–6

Lamb fillets with lentils and spicy eggplant relish

Za'atar is a Middle Eastern spice blend containing sesame seeds, thyme and sumac. Usually mixed with olive oil, it can be drizzled over salads or crumbled feta cheese, or substituted for mixed dried herbs.

ingredients

2 teaspoons olive oil

2 teaspoons garam masala

1 teaspoon za'atar, optional

600 g (1 lb 5 oz) lamb backstraps or loin fillets

250 g (9 oz/1 cup) plain Greek style yoghurt

3 tablespoons finely chopped mint

1 Lebanese (short) cucumber, finely chopped

½ teaspoon sugar

1 tablespoon olive oil, extra

1 teaspoon crushed garlic

2 x 400 g (14 oz) tins lentils, drained and rinsed

spicy eggplant relish

1 tablespoon ground cumin

1 tablespoon ground coriander

1 teaspoon crushed chilli, or to taste

1 teaspoon crushed garlic

3 tablespoons olive oil

500 g (1 lb 2 oz) eggplant (aubergine), chopped

2 tablespoons olive oil, extra

400 g (14 oz) tin chopped tomatoes with juice

2 tablespoons chopped flat-leaf (Italian) parsley

salt, to taste

method

1 Combine the olive oil, garam masala and za'atar in a glass bowl and add the lamb, mixing well to coat. Leave to marinate in the refrigerator for a few hours or overnight.

2 Combine the yoghurt, mint, cucumber and sugar in a bowl and mix well.

3 In a saucepan heat the extra olive oil and cook the garlic briefly then add the lentils. Lower the heat and cook, covered, until heated through. Keep warm.

4 Barbecue the lamb until cooked to your liking. Remove to a plate, cover and rest in a warm place.

5 To serve, cut the lamb into thick slices. Place some spiced lentils onto a plate, top with a few slices of lamb and top that with the yoghurt and mint. Place a large spoonful of **Spicy eggplant relish** on the side.

Serves 4

SPICY EGGPLANT RELISH

Combine the cumin, coriander, chilli, garlic and olive oil in a bowl and mix well. Add the eggplant and toss to coat. Heat the extra olive oil in a frying pan and add the eggplant. Cook over medium–high heat until starting to brown, then lower the heat and stir in the tomatoes. Cover and gently simmer for 10 minutes until soft. Stir through the chopped parsley and season with salt.

Chicken with leek in white wine sauce

Combined with a large bowl of plain rice, steamed potatoes or rice noodles❖, this is a great recipe for serving a crowd or as part of a buffet table.

ingredients

1 tablespoon olive oil
1 leek, white part only, washed well
  and sliced
1 teaspoon crushed garlic
800 g (1 lb 12 oz) boneless, skinless
  chicken breasts, chopped into strips
125 ml (4 fl oz/½ cup) white wine
375 ml (13 fl oz/1½ cups) chicken
  stock❖
2 teaspoons pure maize cornflour
  (cornstarch)
4 thyme sprigs
1 strip of lemon zest
1 tablespoon lemon juice
2 egg yolks
2 tablespoons pouring cream
1 tablespoon chopped flat-leaf (Italian)
  parsley
salt and pepper, to taste

method

1 In a heavy-based saucepan heat the olive oil and cook the leek and garlic until soft. Remove from the pan and set aside in a bowl. Add the chicken strips to the saucepan and cook quickly until browned then place into the bowl with the leeks.

2 Remove the pan from the heat, stir in the wine and stock and scrape up all the browned pieces from the bottom of the pan. Return the pan to the heat, bring to the boil then reduce the heat to very low. Blend the cornflour into 60 ml (2 fl oz/¼ cup) of the hot stock then stir back into the pan.

3 Return the chicken and leek mixture to the pan, add the thyme and lemon zest and simmer gently for 10 minutes until the chicken is tender.

4 In a bowl combine the lemon juice, egg yolks and cream and whisk together.

5 Just before serving remove the pan from the heat, discard the thyme stalks and lemon zest, then stir through the egg mixture and parsley. Don't allow the sauce to boil after adding the yolk mixture as it may curdle — there's plenty of heat left in the pan to cook the egg yolks. Adjust the seasoning with salt and pepper.

6 To serve, place some warmed rice noodles, rice or mashed potato onto a plate, top with a generous spoonful of chicken, with some steamed green beans on the side.

Serves 4

Marinated pork fillet with soy and maple sauce

One ingredient that seems to cause great anxiety is soy sauce, but there's no need to miss out on this wonderful salty condiment. Just make sure you use the brand with gluten free on the label or gluten free tamari.

ingredients

2 pork fillets, about 800 g (1 lb 12 oz)
1 tablespoon olive oil
125 ml (4 fl oz/½ cup) white wine
250 ml (9 fl oz/1 cup) chicken stock❖
1 teaspoon pure maize cornflour
   (cornstarch), optional, for thickening

marinade

3 tablespoons concentrated orange juice
2 tablespoons pure maple syrup
1 tablespoon soy sauce❖
1 tablespoon olive oil
1 teaspoon crushed ginger
1 teaspoon crushed garlic
½ teaspoon Chinese five-spice

method

1 Mix together all the marinade ingredients in a glass or stainless steel bowl. Add the pork and turn to coat evenly in the marinade. Cover and refrigerate overnight.

2 Preheat the oven to 180°C (350°F/Gas 4).

3 Drain the pork fillets. Heat the olive oil in a frying pan over high heat and brown the fillets on all sides. Transfer the pork to an ovenproof dish and roast until cooked to your liking, about 15 minutes, depending on the thickness of the fillets.

4 Remove the pork from the oven, wrap in foil and rest in a warm place for 10 minutes before serving.

5 Meanwhile, deglaze the frying pan with white wine, scraping the brown residue from the bottom of the pan. Add the stock and simmer gently until reduced or, if you prefer, thicken the sauce with the cornflour. Adjust the seasoning if necessary with a little orange juice, soy sauce or maple syrup.

6 Unwrap the pork fillets, adding any accumulated juices to the sauce, then carve into thick slices. Serve with sweet potato and pumpkin (winter squash) mash and stir-fried Asian greens, and drizzle with the sauce

Serves 4

Slow-roasted lamb with sautéed potatoes

ingredients

2 kg (4 lb 8 oz) leg of lamb, bone left in
4 garlic cloves, peeled and sliced
  into slivers
2 teaspoons oregano
2 teaspoons marjoram
2 teaspoons thyme
3 tablespoons lemon juice
grated zest of 1 lemon

sautéed potatoes

500 g (1 lb 2 oz) all-purpose potatoes
1 tablespoon olive oil
1 teaspoon crushed garlic
salt and pepper, to taste

method

1 Preheat oven to 150°C (300°F/Gas 2).
2 With a sharp knife make tiny cuts in the lamb and push a sliver of garlic and some herbs into each cut. Place the lamb into a deep roasting tin or casserole dish, pour over the lemon juice and sprinkle with lemon zest.
3 Cover with foil or a lid and bake for 2 hours. Turn the lamb, baste well then cover and return to the oven for another 1¼ hours. Drain the juices from the tin and bake, uncovered, for another 15–20 minutes or until browned. Remove lamb from the oven, wrap it tightly in foil and rest it in a warm place for 10 minutes before carving.
4 Serve with **Sautéed potatoes** and a **Greek salad**.

Serves 4–6

SAUTÉED POTATOES

Cut the potatoes into chunks and steam until tender. Heat the olive oil in a frying pan, add the garlic and cook briefly then add the potatoes and sauté until browned. Season with salt and pepper.

Roast pumpkin and ricotta lasagne

This will make a large lasagne because there's no point in making a small one. Try some sandwiched on Tannour Bread❖, sprinkled with extra grated parmesan cheese and toasted in a sandwich maker. If possible, make lasagne a day ahead as the texture will be firmer and the flavour better.

ingredients

1 onion, diced

2 tablespoons olive oil

1 teaspoon crushed garlic

500 g (1 lb 2 oz) good-quality minced (ground) beef

60 ml (2 fl oz/¼ cup) red wine

700 g (1 lb 9 oz) bottle tomato passata (pureed tomatoes)

400 g (14 oz) tin chopped tomatoes

¼ teaspoon dried Italian herbs

½ teaspoon sugar

salt and pepper, to taste

250 g (9 oz) packet dried rice paper sheets❖

800 g (1 lb 12 oz) pumpkin (winter squash), peeled and roasted

375 g (13 oz/1½ cups) ricotta cheese

white sauce

40 g (1½ oz) butter

2 tablespoons pure maize cornflour (cornstarch)

500 ml (17 fl oz/2 cups) milk

25 g (1 oz/¼ cup) grated parmesan cheese

salt, to taste

method

1 Grease a 5 cm (2 in) deep, 33 x 23 cm (13 x 9 in) ovenproof dish.

2 To make the bolognese sauce, in a large saucepan sweat the onion in olive oil over low heat until soft. Increase the heat and add the garlic and beef. Break up any lumps in the meat and cook until well browned. Reduce the heat and add the red wine, tomato passata, chopped tomatoes, herbs and sugar. Reduce the heat to very low and simmer for 30–40 minutes or until the sauce looks rich and dark. Season with salt and pepper. When cooled, puree the sauce with a hand blender for a finer texture.

3 Preheat oven to 180°C (350°F/Gas 4).

4 To soften the rice paper sheets, fill a large bowl with very hot water, soak a few sheets at a time until soft, then drain on a clean tea towel (dish towel). Repeat with as many sheets as needed. I usually use a double layer of sheets in lasagne.

5 Ladle some bolognese sauce into the bottom of the baking tin then top with some softened rice paper sheets.

6 In a separate bowl roughly mash the roast pumpkin and mix in the ricotta. Spread over the rice sheets and top with another layer of softened rice sheets. Ladle some more bolognese sauce on top and cover with another layer of softened rice sheets.

7 To make the white sauce, in a saucepan over medium heat melt the butter and stir in the cornflour. Cook for 1–2 minutes then add the milk. Stir until the sauce is almost boiling, then reduce the heat and simmer gently. Stir in the parmesan cheese and season with salt.

8 Spoon the white sauce over the lasagne and bake in the oven for about 1 hour or until browned on top and heated through.

9 To serve, reheat the lasagne if necessary, cut into large squares and serve with a mixed salad with red onions, and offer extra grated parmesan cheese.

Serves 8

Mellow beef and red wine casserole

ingredients

olive oil

250 g (9 oz) French shallots, peeled and halved, or quartered if large

125 g (4½ oz) rindless bacon slices, cut into small matchsticks

1 teaspoon crushed garlic

500 ml (17 fl oz/2 cups) beef stock❖

1 kg (2 lb 4 oz) trimmed blade or chuck steak, cubed

250 ml (9 fl oz/1 cup) red wine (cabernet or shiraz)

100 ml (3½ fl oz) port

1 tablespoon pure maize cornflour (cornstarch)

2 carrots, peeled and cut into chunks

2 generous tablespoons tomato paste (concentrated puree)

1 bay leaf

2 thyme sprigs, leaves only

250 g (9 oz) Swiss brown mushrooms, halved, or quartered if large

method

1 Preheat the oven to 150°C (300°F/Gas 2).

2 Heat a little olive oil in a large casserole dish and fry the shallots until soft then remove to a bowl. Increase the heat, add the bacon and fry until browned. Add the garlic when the bacon is nearly ready. Remove the garlic and bacon to the bowl with the shallots.

3 Pour the beef stock into the casserole dish and stir it around the dish, scraping up all the browned bits then pour this into the bowl with the bacon and shallots.

4 Heat some more olive oil in the casserole dish and brown the meat in batches over high heat. Remove the meat from the dish, lower the heat and stir in the red wine and port, again stirring up the residue. Remove about 60 ml (2 fl oz/¼ cup) of liquid, blend in the cornflour then stir back into the dish and simmer. Return the cooked items to the casserole dish and add the carrots, tomato paste and herbs. Mix together, adding a little more stock if necessary to cover.

5 Cover the casserole with a lid and transfer to the oven and cook for 2–2½ hours until the meat is very tender. Stir a few times during the cooking and add the mushrooms for the last 30 minutes.

6 Remove the bay leaf, check the seasoning and serve with garlic mashed potatoes and steamed green beans.

Serves 4–6

Butter kisses

ingredients

60 g (2¼ oz/½ cup) white rice flour
85 g (3 oz/⅔ cup) pure maize cornflour
(cornstarch)
35 g (1¼ oz/¼ cup) custard powder❖
½ teaspoon baking powder❖
½ teaspoon xanthan gum
125 g (4½ oz) butter, softened
115 g (4 oz/½ cup) caster (superfine)
sugar
1 egg
pure icing (confectioners') sugar, extra

butter cream

125 g (4½ oz) butter, softened
185 g (6½ oz/1½ cups) pure icing
(confectioners') sugar, sifted
1 tablespoon milk
2 drops red food colouring, optional

method

1 Preheat oven to 200°C (400°F/Gas 6).
2 Line four baking trays with baking paper.
3 In a bowl combine the rice flour, cornflour, custard powder, baking powder and xanthan gum and stir to combine.
4 In a separate bowl beat the butter and caster sugar together until light and creamy, then add the egg and beat until well combined. Stir in the dry ingredients — it will seem a little dry to begin with.
5 Spoon the mixture into a piping bag or a plastic bag with the corner cut off and pipe 2 cm (¾ in) rounds onto the prepared baking trays. Try not to make the biscuits too big as they spread during baking and are quite rich.
6 Bake for 8–10 minutes or until light golden. Rest the biscuits on the trays for a few minutes then place onto wire racks to cool, pairing up sizes as you go.
7 Join the cold biscuits together with a generous amount of **Butter cream** and dust with extra pure icing sugar.

Makes about 24 kisses

BUTTER CREAM

Beat the butter with an electric mixer until very pale then add the icing sugar and milk. Add the food colouring if using, and mix until smooth.

132 |GLUTEN FREE AND EASY |SOMETHING SWEET

Almond biscotti

The term 'glutinous' rice flour is a little misleading as it has nothing to do with gluten but is flour from a sweet, sticky type of rice used in Asian cooking. It's available from the Asian food section of supermarkets.

ingredients

210 g (7½ oz/1½ cups) **Rice flour blend**
1 tablespoon glutinous rice flour
2 teaspoons baking powder❖
1 teaspoon xanthan gum
65 g (2¼ oz) butter, softened
115 g (4 oz/½ cup) soft brown sugar
2 tablespoons white corn syrup
1 teaspoon natural vanilla extract
½ teaspoon almond essence
2 eggs
60 g (2¼ oz/½ cup) slivered almonds, toasted and chopped

method

1 Preheat oven to 170°C (325°F/Gas 3).
2 Line a large baking tray with baking paper.
3 Combine the flours, baking powder and xanthan gum in a bowl and mix well. In a separate bowl beat the butter and sugar together then add the corn syrup, vanilla and almond essence and beat until smooth. Add the eggs one at a time, beating well in between. Combine the dry ingredients with the butter mixture and then stir in the almonds.
4 Using two spatulas, form the dough into three logs on the prepared baking tray. Leave plenty of room for spreading and don't worry about getting things too neat as the surface will smooth out during baking.
5 Bake for 20 minutes or until lightly browned and cooked through when tested with a cake skewer. Let the logs firm up on the baking tray for a few minutes then remove to a wire rack to cool.
6 When cooled, cut the loaves into 7–8 mm (³⁄₈ in) slices with a serrated knife. Lay the biscuits flat on the baking tray and bake again until the biscuits are crisp, about 7–10 minutes. The longer you bake them at this stage the harder they'll become.
7 Gently remove the biscotti to a wire rack to cool.

Makes about 2 dozen

Rosewater shortbread

ingredients

125 g (4½ oz) butter, softened
125 g (4½ oz/1 cup) pure icing
   (confectioners') sugar, sifted
1 egg
1 teaspoon rosewater
180 g (6 oz/1½ cups) white rice
   flour, sifted
pure icing (confectioners') sugar, extra

method

1 Beat the butter and icing sugar until pale then add the
   egg and rosewater and beat well. Add the sifted flour
   and beat until the mixture is smooth. Cover and
   refrigerate overnight.
2 Preheat oven to 180°C (350°F/Gas 4).
3 Line two baking trays with baking paper.
4 Roll the mixture into little balls and flatten slightly, or place
   into a piping bag and pipe small shapes onto the
   prepared trays, allowing room for the biscuits to spread.
   Bake for 8 minutes or until just starting to colour.
5 Leave the shortbread to set on the trays for a few minutes
   then remove to wire racks to cool.
6 Dust with extra pure icing sugar to serve.

Makes about 30

Marmalade friands

ingredients

40 g (1½ oz/⅓ cup) white rice flour
125 g (4½ oz/1¼ cups) ground almonds
125 g (4½ oz/1 cup) pure icing
   (confectioners') sugar, sifted
zest of 1 orange, finely chopped
5 egg whites, whisked until frothy
125 g (4½ oz) butter, melted and cooled
80 g (2¾ oz/¼ cup) marmalade jam

method

1 Preheat oven to 180°C (350°F/Gas 4).
2 Grease eight friand moulds or patty tins.
3 In a bowl sift together the rice flour, ground almonds
   and icing sugar. Add the chopped orange zest then stir
   in the egg whites, followed by the melted butter. Spoon
   the batter into the prepared moulds until they are about
   three-quarters full.
4 Bake for 25 minutes (less for the patty tins) until golden
   and cooked through. Allow the friands to firm up in the
   moulds for a few minutes before turning out to cool on
   a wire rack, right way up.
5 Heat the marmalade in the microwave until melted then
   brush the tops of the warm friands with the melted jam
   and allow to cool.

Makes 8 friands

Chocolate madeleines

ingredients

70 g (2½ oz/½ cup) **Rice flour blend**
2 tablespoons unsweetened cocoa
  powder
20 g (¾ oz/¼ cup) ground almonds
¼ teaspoon xanthan gum
pinch of salt
3 eggs
80 g (2¾ oz/⅓ cup) caster (superfine)
  sugar
½ teaspoon natural vanilla extract
1 teaspoon plain Greek style yoghurt
100 g (3½ oz) butter, melted and cooled
pure icing (confectioners') sugar

method

1 Preheat oven to 170°C (325°F/Gas 3), fan-forced
  if possible.
2 Grease a madeleine tin or patty tin.
3 In a bowl sift together the flour, cocoa powder, ground
  almonds, xanthan gum and salt. In a separate bowl beat
  the eggs, sugar, vanilla and yoghurt until thick and pale.
  Stir in the dry ingredients then add the melted butter and
  beat only until all the ingredients are incorporated.
4 Pour dessertspoons of mixture into the prepared tin and
  bake for 7–8 minutes until just cooked through. Allow the
  madeleines to set in the tin for a few minutes then
  carefully remove to a wire rack to cool, shell side up.
5 Dust with icing sugar to serve.

Makes about 20

Carrot and pecan cake

ingredients

200 g (7 oz/2 cups) pecan nuts

95 g (3½ oz/⅔ cup) **Rice flour blend**

6 eggs, separated

1 teaspoon natural vanilla extract

285 g (10 oz/1¼ cups) caster (superfine) sugar

2 large sweet carrots, finely grated, about 300 g (10½ oz/2 cups)

1 teaspoon baking powder✤

1 teaspoon mixed spice

pinch of salt

pure icing (confectioners') sugar, to serve

method

1 Preheat oven to 170°C (325°F/Gas 3).

2 Grease a 24 cm (9½ in) ring (Bundt) tin.

3 Process the pecans and flour in a food processor until the nuts are finely ground.

4 In a large bowl beat the egg yolks, vanilla and sugar until pale then stir in the grated carrot and mix well. Add the nut and flour mixture, baking powder, mixed spice and salt and combine well.

5 In a separate bowl beat the egg whites to soft peak stage then fold half into the cake mixture. When all the egg white is incorporated, add the remaining egg white and mix thoroughly.

6 Pour the batter into the prepared tin. Bake for 45 minutes or until risen and evenly browned. Allow the cake to firm up in the tin for at least 20 minutes then turn out onto a wire rack to cool.

7 To serve, simply dust with pure icing sugar.

Serves 8–10

Orange and almond cake

Choose oranges with unblemished skins as the whole fruit is used in this recipe.

ingredients

2 large navel oranges, washed
5 eggs
285 g (10 oz/1¼ cups) caster (superfine)
    sugar
250 g (9 oz/2½ cups) ground almonds
1 teaspoon baking powder❖
pure icing (confectioners') sugar,
    to serve

variations

✤ Add 1 tablespoon poppy seeds.
✤ As a dessert, serve with **Oranges in toffee syrup** and a little cream.
✤ Substitute 3 medium mandarins for the oranges.

method

1 Preheat oven to 170°C (325°F/Gas 3).
2 Grease and line the base of eight small heart-shaped tins or one 24 cm (9½ in) spring-form tin.
3 Place the two whole oranges in a saucepan and cover with water. Bring to the boil and simmer, covered, for 1 hour, ensuring that the oranges remain covered with water. Drain and cool. Chop the oranges into quarters, discard any seeds then place the chunks into a blender and puree until smooth.
4 Beat the eggs with the sugar until thick then add the orange puree, ground almonds and baking powder and mix well.
5 Pour into the prepared tins and bake for 25 minutes for the small tins and 1 hour for the large tin. Leave the cake to firm up in the tin for 20 minutes then turn out onto a wire rack, remove the baking paper and flip over to finish cooling, right way up. This cake definitely mellows with a little time and can be prepared up to 48 hours in advance.
6 To serve, sift icing sugar on top. You can also decorate with orange zest and flaked almonds if desired.

Serves 8

Chocolate and coffee layer cake

I made two of these cakes, one with coffee cream and the other with raspberry cream, but couldn't decide which one to use as the main recipe, so we ate both — purely for research of course! For the record, Libby preferred the raspberry cream.

ingredients

70 g (2½ oz/½ cup) **Rice flour blend**
2 tablespoons unsweetened cocoa
   powder
1 teaspoon baking powder❖
¼ teaspoon xanthan gum
3 eggs
115 g (4 oz/½ cup) caster (superfine)
   sugar
1 tablespoon plain Greek style yoghurt

coffee cream

125 g (4½ oz) mascarpone
125 ml (4 fl oz/½ cup) thickened
   (whipping) cream
2 tablespoons pure icing (confectioners')
   sugar, sifted
1 tablespoon instant espresso
   coffee powder

ganache

100 ml (3½ fl oz) pouring cream
100 g (3½ oz) dark chocolate, chopped

method

1 Preheat oven to 180°C (350°F/Gas 4).
2 Grease and line the base of a 3 cm (1½ in) deep, 30 x 23 cm (12 x 9 in) baking tin.
3 To make the cake, in a bowl sift together the flour, cocoa powder, baking powder and xanthan gum.
4 In a separate bowl beat the eggs and sugar until thick and pale then add the yoghurt and gently fold in the dry ingredients. Spoon mixture into the tin and bake for 15 minutes or until cooked through. Allow the cake to cool and firm up in the tin, then turn out onto a wire rack and remove the baking paper.
5 When completely cooled, cut the cake in half horizontally and spread one half with **Coffee cream**. Place the other half on top and spread with **Ganache**.

Serves 6–8

COFFEE CREAM

In a bowl whisk together the mascarpone, cream, icing sugar and coffee powder until smooth and thick.

GANACHE

In a saucepan bring the cream just to the boil. Process the chocolate in a food processor until it is in small pieces then add the cream and process until smooth. Stand the mixture at room temperature for a few minutes to thicken.

Chocolate and raspberry layer cake

To make this variation, proceed as above but replace the coffee cream with raspberry cream. To make the raspberry cream, whisk 125 g (4½ oz) mascarpone, 125 ml (4 fl oz/½ cup) thickened (whipping) cream and 2 tablespoons pure icing (confectioners') sugar until smooth and thick then gently fold in 100 g (3½ oz) fresh raspberries.

Macadamia cake

ingredients

80 g (2¾ oz/½ cup) unsalted
   macadamia nuts
60 g (2¼ oz/½ cup) white rice flour
40 g (1½ oz/¼ cup) potato starch
30 g (1 oz/¼ cup) pure maize
   cornflour (cornstarch)
230 g (8 oz/1 cup) caster (superfine)
   sugar
125 g (4½ oz) butter, softened
3 eggs, separated
2 teaspoons baking powder❖
½ teaspoon xanthan gum
60 g (2¼ oz/¼ cup) plain Greek style
   yoghurt
110 g (3¾ oz/2 cups) flaked or
   shredded coconut

butter cream

100 g (3½ oz) butter, extra, softened
125 g (4½ oz/1 cup) pure icing
   (confectioners') sugar, sifted
1 tablespoon milk
¼ teaspoon natural vanilla extract

method

1 Preheat oven to 170°C (325°F/Gas 3).
2 Grease and line the base of a 20 cm (8 in) spring-form tin.
3 Place the macadamia nuts, rice flour, potato starch and cornflour into a food processor and process until the nuts are finely ground.
4 Beat together the caster sugar and butter until fluffy then add the egg yolks and beat well. Add the flour and nut mixture, baking powder and xanthan gum, mix well then stir in the yoghurt.
5 In a separate bowl beat the egg whites to soft peak stage then fold into the butter mixture.
6 Spoon the batter into the prepared tin and bake for about 50 minutes or until a skewer inserted into the middle of the cake comes out clean. Leave the cake to set in the tin for 10 minutes, then turn out to cool on a wire rack, right side up. When fully cooled, spread **Butter cream** over the top and side of the cake and decorate with coconut.

Serves 6–8

BUTTER CREAM

Beat the extra butter until pale, add the icing sugar, milk and vanilla and mix well.

Pistachio and apple cake

ingredients

100 g (3½ oz/⅔ cup) shelled, unsalted
    pistachio nuts
30 g (1 oz/¼ cup) white rice flour
½ teaspoon baking powder❖
150 g (5½ oz/1½ cups) ground almonds
6 eggs, separated
115 g (4 oz/½ cup) caster (superfine)
    sugar
115 g (4 oz/½ cup) caster (superfine)
    sugar, extra
50 g (1¾ oz) apple, such as Fuji,
    unpeeled and grated
50 g (1¾ oz) butter, melted

to serve

pure icing (confectioners') sugar
sweetened mascarpone
shredded mint

method

1 Preheat oven to 180°C (350°F/Gas 4).
2 Grease and line the base of a 26 cm (10½ in) spring-form
   tin.
3 Place the pistachio nuts and flour in a food processor and
   process until the nuts are finely ground. The flour helps
   the nuts to grind evenly. Add the baking powder and
   ground almonds and pulse until just combined.
4 Using an electric mixer beat the egg yolks and the first lot
   of sugar on high speed until the mixture is very thick. Add
   the nut and flour mixture, apple and butter and stir well.
   The mixture will be quite stiff at this stage.
5 In a separate bowl beat the egg whites to soft peak stage
   then add the extra sugar and beat to firm peak stage.
   Gently fold the egg whites into the nut mixture
   in two batches. Place the mixture into the prepared tin
   and bake for 50–60 minutes or until cooked through.
   Allow the cake to set in the tin for 10 minutes then turn
   out onto a wire rack to cool.
6 To serve, dust the cake with pure icing sugar and serve
   slices with a dollop of mascarpone and a little mint.

Serves 8

Lemon tea cake with lemon butter

If cutting the cake into layers seems fraught with danger, just skip that part and serve the **Lemon butter** separately. The butter can be made a day ahead and kept refrigerated until needed.

ingredients

210 g (7½ oz/1½ cups) **Rice flour blend**
2 teaspoons baking powder❖
1 teaspoon bicarbonate of soda
   (baking soda)
1 teaspoon xanthan gum
¼ teaspoon salt
125 g (4½ oz) butter, softened
230 g (8 oz/1 cup) caster (superfine)
   sugar
3 large eggs
2 tablespoons finely chopped lemon
   zest, about 2 lemons
2 tablespoons lemon juice
1 teaspoon natural vanilla extract
125 g (4½ oz/½ cup) plain Greek style
   yoghurt
pure icing (confectioners') sugar,
   to serve

method

1 Preheat oven to 170°C (325°F/Gas 3).
2 Grease a non-stick, 22 x 28 cm (8½ x 11¼ in) baking tin.
3 In a bowl sift together the flour, baking powder, bicarbonate of soda, xanthan gum and salt.
4 In a separate large bowl beat the butter and sugar together until pale then add the eggs one at a time, beating well between each. Beat in the lemon zest, lemon juice and vanilla. Beat in the dry ingredients alternately with the yoghurt.
5 Place the batter into the prepared tin and bake for 30–35 minutes until cooked through in the centre. Allow the cake to firm up in the tin for about 10 minutes then turn out to cool on a wire rack.
6 When fully cooled, split the cake into two layers and spread the bottom layer with **Lemon butter**. Replace the top and sprinkle with sifted pure icing sugar to serve.

Serves 8

LEMON BUTTER

Place 2 large eggs and 80 g (2¾ oz/⅓ cup) caster (superfine) sugar into the top of a double boiler and whisk until blended. Add 80 ml (2½ fl oz/⅓ cup) lemon juice and 60 g (2¼ oz) butter, chopped into pieces. Place over simmering water and whisk until the mixture thickens and lightens in colour. Pour into a bowl and cool then press plastic wrap onto the surface, cover the bowl and refrigerate.

Makes about 160 g (5½ oz/²⁄₃ cup)

Caramelized figs

ingredients
60 ml (2 fl oz/¼ cup) water
185 g (6½ oz/1 cup) soft brown sugar
1 tablespoon butter
6 figs, halved

to serve
sweetened mascarpone

method

1 In a saucepan over medium heat combine the water and brown sugar and stir until the sugar dissolves. Simmer for 5 minutes.

2 Melt the butter in a large frying pan then add the figs, cut side down, and cook briefly. Pour the sugar syrup over the figs and cook over low heat until the syrup has caramelized.

3 To serve place 3 fig halves onto individual plates, spoon over some of the syrup and serve with a little sweetened mascarpone on the side.

Serves 4

Oranges in toffee syrup

ingredients

4 oranges
230 g (8 oz/1 cup) caster (superfine)
   sugar
125 ml (4 fl oz/½ cup) water
125 ml (4 fl oz/½ cup) water, extra
1 tablespoon Cointreau

method

1 Peel the oranges thickly, leaving no white pith. Slice and place into a large bowl.
2 Place the sugar and water into a saucepan and stir over medium heat to dissolve. Once the sugar is dissolved, increase the heat and boil, without stirring, until the syrup is a light golden colour. Remove the pan from the heat and add the extra water, taking care as the syrup will spit a little. Return the pan to the heat and stir to dissolve the toffee, then remove from the heat and leave to cool. Stir in the Cointreau.
3 Half an hour before serving, pour the toffee syrup over the oranges.
4 Serve with sweetened mascarpone or as an accompaniment to **Orange and almond cake**.

Serves 4

Poached pears with caramel sauce

These pears can be made a day or two ahead and stored covered in the refrigerator. I like them served warm so I give them a brief zap in the microware on medium.

ingredients

500 ml (17 fl oz/2 cups) apple juice
750 ml (26 fl oz/3 cups) water or more
110 g (3¾ oz/½ cup) sugar
1 strip of orange peel
1 teaspoon lemon juice
1 cinnamon stick
4 firm ripe pears, peeled but
    retaining stems

caramel sauce

220 g (7¾ oz/1 cup) sugar
60 ml (2 fl oz/¼ cup) water
125 ml (4 fl oz/½ cup) pouring cream
1 teaspoon lemon juice
1 tablespoon butter, chopped

variation

For a lighter sauce try toffee syrup. Place 230 g (8 oz/1 cup) caster (superfine) sugar into a saucepan with 125 ml (4 fl oz/½ cup) water and stir until dissolved. Bring to the boil and boil rapidly, uncovered, until golden, then remove from the heat and stir in 125 ml (4 fl oz/½ cup) of the reserved poaching liquid. Return to the heat and stir until the toffee is dissolved.

method

1 In a saucepan large enough to fit the pears snugly combine the apple juice, water, sugar, orange peel, lemon juice and cinnamon stick. Add the pears, increasing the amount of water if necessary to cover.

2 Cut a circle of baking paper to fit the saucepan and cover the pears to help prevent them browning. Bring to the boil then reduce heat and simmer gently for 15–20 minutes until tender. Remove from heat and allow the pears to cool in the poaching liquid. When cool, remove the pears and reserve 125 ml (4 fl oz/½ cup) of the poaching liquid.

3 Serve the pears warm or at room temperature drizzled with warm **Caramel sauce** with sweetened mascarpone or cream on the side.

Serves 4

CARAMEL SAUCE

Place the sugar and water in a saucepan and stir over medium heat until the sugar is dissolved. Increase the heat and boil rapidly, without stirring, until a rich golden colour. Remove the pan from the heat and stir in the cream. The mixture will bubble up and look like it's all gone wrong but return the pan to the heat and stir until the caramel is smooth. Add the lemon juice and butter and stir until the sauce is of a thick pouring consistency, adding a little of the poaching liquid to thin if necessary.

Luscious little lemon puddings

ingredients

4 eggs

145 g (5 oz/^{2}/$_3$ cup) caster (superfine)
  sugar

125 ml (4 fl oz/^{1}/$_2$ cup) lemon juice

1 tablespoon finely chopped lemon zest

125 ml (4 fl oz/^{1}/$_2$ cup) pouring cream

pure icing (confectioners') sugar,
  to serve

method

1 Preheat oven to 160°C (315°F/Gas 2–3).

2 Prepare a water bath.

3 Whisk eggs and sugar until thick. Stir in the juice and
  zest and gently whisk in the cream. Pour into four 125 ml
  (4 fl oz/^{1}/$_2$ cup) ramekins and bake in the water bath for
  20–25 minutes or until just set. Remove the puddings
  and cool then cover and refrigerate until needed.

4 Serve puddings at room temperature, dusted with
  icing sugar.

Serves 4

Crème caramel

This is the easiest dessert and always looks like you went to a lot more effort than you actually did. Technically there is enough custard here to make six 150 ml (5 fl oz) desserts but I'm sticking with the 'Serves 4' because I like a big serving.

ingredients

230 g (8 oz/1 cup) caster (superfine) sugar
80 ml (2½ fl oz/⅓ cup) water
3 eggs
2 egg yolks
55 g (2 oz/¼ cup) caster (superfine) sugar, extra
½ teaspoon natural vanilla extract
375 ml (13 fl oz/1½ cups) pouring cream
500 ml (17 fl oz/2 cups) milk

variations

✳ Rosewater crème caramel: Replace vanilla with 2 teaspoons rosewater.
✳ Coconut crème caramel: Replace milk and cream with coconut cream.

method

1 Preheat oven to 150°C (300°F/Gas 2).
2 Have ready four 250 ml (9 fl oz/1 cup) ramekins or one large round soufflé dish.
3 Prepare a water bath.
4 In a saucepan bring the sugar and water to the boil, stirring until the sugar is dissolved. Allow to boil, without stirring, until it starts to turn a golden colour. Remove from the heat and pour a small amount of toffee into each ramekin, swirling to coat the base.
5 Place the ramekins into a large baking tin.
6 Whisk the eggs, egg yolks, extra sugar and vanilla until well combined. Bring the cream and milk just to the boil then whisk into the egg mixture. Pour the custard into the ramekins.
7 Put the ramekins into the baking tin and gently pour boiling water into the tin around the ramekins. Carefully place the baking tin into the oven. Bake until the custards are only just set, about 30 minutes, or slightly longer if using the larger dish.
8 Remove ramekins from the water, cool to room temperature then cover and refrigerate overnight.
9 Remove from the refrigerator at least 10 minutes before serving, gently run a knife around the sides and invert onto serving plates.

Serves 4–6

Pavlova

The addition of cornflour and vinegar transforms a simple meringue into a crisp-on-the-outside, marshmallow-on-the-inside pavlova.

ingredients

4 egg whites
230 g (8 oz/1 cup) caster (superfine) sugar
1 tablespoon pure maize cornflour (cornstarch)
1 teaspoon white vinegar
few drops natural vanilla extract

to serve

sweetened thickened (whipping) cream and fruit

method

1 Preheat oven to 120°C (230°F/Gas ½).
2 Line a baking tray with baking paper and draw a 20–22 cm (8–8½ in) circle on the back of the paper.
3 In a clean glass bowl, using electric beaters, beat the egg whites to soft peak stage. Add one-third of the sugar and beat on high speed until all of the sugar is dissolved. Gradually add the rest of the sugar and beat until fully dissolved and the mixture is shiny. Fold in the cornflour, followed by the vinegar and a few drops of vanilla.
4 Pile the meringue inside the circle on the prepared baking tray and flatten the top slightly.
5 Bake for about 1¼ hours until the pavlova is dry and crisp. Turn the oven off but leave the pavlova in the oven with the door ajar to cool completely.
6 To keep the shell crisp, decorate with cream and fruit just before serving.

Serves 6–8

To increase or decrease a pavlova, the ratio is 55 g (2 oz/¼ cup) caster sugar per medium egg white.

Individual brown sugar meringues with praline cream

ingredients

2 egg whites
95 g (3½ oz/½ cup) soft brown sugar
½ teaspoon white vinegar

praline cream

100 g (3½ oz/⅔ cup) blanched almonds
170 g (6 oz/¾ cup) caster (superfine) sugar
125 ml (4 fl oz/½ cup) water
200 g (7 oz) ricotta cheese
60 g (2¼ oz/½ cup) pure icing (confectioners') sugar, sifted
185 ml (6 fl oz/¾ cup) thickened (whipping) cream

method

1 Preheat oven to 120°C (230°F/Gas ½).
2 Line two baking trays with baking paper and draw eight 8 cm (3¼ in) circles.
3 In a clean glass bowl, using electric beaters, beat the egg whites to soft peak stage then add half the brown sugar and beat until dissolved. Add the rest of the brown sugar and beat until smooth. Using a rubber spatula gently fold in the vinegar then drop the meringue onto the lined trays and spread to evenly fill the circles. Keep them on the small side as they spread a little while baking.
4 Bake for 1¼–1½ hours until the meringues are dry and cooked through. Turn the oven off but leave the meringues in the oven with the door ajar to cool. When fully cooled carefully remove the meringues to an airtight container.
5 To serve, place one meringue on a serving plate and top with a dollop of **Praline cream**. Decorate with a few larger pieces of praline.

Makes 8 meringues

PRALINE CREAM

Toast the almonds in a hot, dry frying pan until browned, keeping the nuts moving to prevent them burning. Remove and cool then spread onto a non-stick baking tray. Combine the caster sugar and water in a small saucepan and stir over low heat until the sugar dissolves. Increase the heat and boil, without stirring, until the toffee is a deep golden colour, then immediately pour over the nuts and allow to set. Break praline into smallish pieces, reserving a few pieces for decoration, then place the rest in a food processor and process until fine. Set aside and rinse out the bowl. In the food processor, process the ricotta and icing sugar until mixed. With the motor running, pour the cream in through the feed tube and process only until smooth. Remove to a bowl and stir in the praline.

Upside-down toffee apple cake

Whatever you do, don't make this in a spring-form cake tin — I speak from personal experience.

ingredients

145 g (5 oz/$^2/_3$ cup) caster (superfine)
   sugar
60 ml (2 fl oz/$^1/_4$ cup) water
60 ml (2 fl oz/$^1/_4$ cup) boiling water
3 cooking apples, such as Fuji
125 g ($4^1/_2$ oz) butter, softened
125 g ($4^1/_2$ oz/$^2/_3$ cup) soft brown sugar
2 eggs
60 g ($2^1/_4$ oz/$^1/_4$ cup) plain Greek
   style yoghurt
140 g (5 oz/1 cup) **Rice flour blend**
2 teaspoons baking powder❖
$^1/_2$ teaspoon xanthan gum
1 teaspoon cinnamon
$^1/_2$ teaspoon ground ginger
55 g (2 oz/$^1/_2$ cup) ground almonds

method

1 Preheat oven to 180°C (350°F/Gas 4).
2 Grease and line the base of a deep 24 cm ($9^1/_2$ in) cake tin, or a 21 cm ($8^1/_4$ in) ovenproof mixing bowl.
3 Place the caster sugar and water into a saucepan and stir over low heat until the sugar dissolves. Increase the heat and boil, without stirring, until the toffee is a good golden colour. Immediately remove the pan from the heat and put in the sink. Carefully add the boiling water and stand back while the toffee bubbles up. When the mixture settles, stir the toffee to blend then pour into the base of the cake tin.
4 Peel, core and chop the apples and pile on top of the toffee in the cake tin.
5 Beat the butter and brown sugar until thick then beat in the eggs one at a time, and stir in the yoghurt.
6 In a separate bowl sift the dry ingredients together, add the ground almonds then stir into the butter mixture.
7 Gently and evenly spoon the batter over the apples and bake for 45–50 minutes until the cake is cooked in the centre. Leave to set in the tin for 10 minutes then turn out onto a serving plate and remove the baking paper.
8 Serve the cake warm as a dessert, with **Vanilla custard** or cream.

Serves 8

Vanilla custard

In a saucepan bring 310 ml ($10^3/_4$ fl oz/$1^1/_4$ cups) milk and 1 split vanilla bean to a very gentle simmer. Remove from the heat, pour into a bowl and set aside for 10 minutes to infuse. Rinse out the saucepan. In a separate bowl whisk together 3 large egg yolks, 2 tablespoons caster (superfine) sugar and a pinch of salt until frothy. Pour the warm milk through a strainer into the egg yolk mixture and whisk to combine. Return to the saucepan and cook over low heat until the custard thickens, stirring constantly. When thickened, strain the custard into a clean bowl and cool, covered, stirring a few times. Press plastic wrap onto the surface, cover with a lid and store for up to 3 days in the refrigerator.
Makes 310 ml ($10^3/_4$ fl oz/$1^1/_4$ cups)

Baby cheesecakes with blackberry sauce

I make these in a Texas-size muffin tin but that's just my sweet tooth showing. If you use the regular size tins you'll make about eight.

ingredients

120 g (4¼ oz/1 cup) ground Rice Ring Cookies❖
40 g (1½ oz) butter, melted
375 g (13 oz) plain cream cheese, softened
80 g (2¾ oz/⅓ cup) caster (superfine) sugar
½ teaspoon natural vanilla extract
2 large eggs
2 large egg yolks

blackberry sauce

55 g (2 oz/¼ cup) sugar
125 ml (4 fl oz/½ cup) apple juice
225 g (8 oz) blackberries
1 teaspoon pure maize cornflour (cornstarch)

method

1 Preheat oven to 170°C (325°F/Gas 3).
2 Line the bases of a non-stick muffin tin.
3 Prepare a water bath.
4 Combine the biscuit crumbs and butter in a bowl and mix well. Press a tablespoon of mixture into the bottom of each muffin hole and press down with your fingers to form the base.
5 In a large bowl, using electric beaters, beat the cream cheese, sugar and vanilla until fluffy. Add the eggs and egg yolks and beat well, scraping down the side of the bowl. Place the mixture into the muffin tin and smooth the tops.
6 Place the tin in the water bath and bake for 25–30 minutes until set. Remove from the water bath and cool. Cover with plastic wrap and refrigerate for 6 hours or overnight to firm up. If left overnight these little cheesecakes will easily slip out of the tin.
7 To serve, remove the baking paper, place a cheesecake onto a serving plate and drizzle with warm **Blackberry sauce**.

Makes 4 jumbo, 6 Texas or 8 regular

BLACKBERRY SAUCE

Place the sugar, juice and half the blackberries into a saucepan and stir over medium heat to dissolve the sugar. Bring to the boil then reduce the heat and simmer until the berries release their juices. In a small bowl dissolve the cornflour in 1 tablespoon of the juice and then stir back into the sauce. Simmer, stirring, for another few minutes until the sauce thickens. Remove from the heat, add the remaining blackberries and stir until heated through.

Flourless chocolate cake

Anyone who's rude enough to point out the cracks on top doesn't get any!

ingredients

200 g (7 oz) butter

200 g (7 oz) dark chocolate

6 eggs, separated

230 g (8 oz/1 cup) caster (superfine) sugar

pure icing (confectioners') sugar or unsweetened cocoa powder, to serve

method

1 Preheat oven to 180°C (350°F/Gas 4).

2 Grease and line the base of a 26 cm (10½ in) spring-form tin.

3 Place the butter and chocolate in the top of a double boiler and stir over gently simmering water until melted. Allow to cool.

4 Beat the egg yolks and sugar until thick then add the chocolate mixture and stir until fully combined.

5 In a clean glass or metal bowl, using electric beaters, beat the egg whites to stiff peak stage. Place half the egg white into the chocolate mixture and fold in gently until combined. Repeat with the remaining egg white.

6 Pour the mixture into the prepared tin and bake for 45 minutes or until set in the middle. Allow the cake to cool and firm up in the tin — it will fall back dramatically, leaving a higher rim around the outside and with a few cracks on the surface but it's supposed to look like that!

7 When cooled, gently turn out, remove the baking paper and place onto a serving plate, right way up.

8 To serve, dust with pure icing sugar or cocoa powder.

Serves 8–10

Blueberry dessert cake

To make both the cake and the **Blueberry sauce**, you'll need a total of 300 g (10½ oz) of blueberries. If you can't find fresh blueberries use frozen rather than tinned.

ingredients

70 g (2½ oz) blueberries
1½ tablespoons caster (superfine) sugar
zest of 1 orange, finely chopped
95 g (3½ oz/⅔ cup) **Rice flour blend**
60 g (2¼ oz/⅓ cup) polenta
80 g (2¾ oz/¾ cup) ground almonds
2 teaspoons baking powder❖
1 teaspoon xanthan gum
¼ teaspoon salt
3 whole eggs plus 1 egg white
80 g (2¾ oz/⅓ cup) caster (superfine)
    sugar, extra
100 g (3½ oz) butter, melted
60 ml (2 fl oz/¼ cup) buttermilk
65 g (2¼ oz/¼ cup) apple puree

blueberry sauce

55 g (2 oz/¼ cup) sugar
1 tablespoon orange juice
225 g (8 oz/1½ cups) blueberries
1 teaspoon pure maize cornflour
    (cornstarch)

method

1 Preheat oven to 180°C.
2 Grease and line a 24 cm (9½ in) spring-form tin.
3 Combine the blueberries, sugar and orange zest in a small saucepan over low heat, and stir until the sugar has melted in the berry juice. Remove from the heat.
4 In a bowl combine the flour, polenta, ground almonds, baking powder, xanthan gum and salt and mix well.
5 In a separate bowl beat together the eggs, egg white, extra sugar, melted butter, buttermilk and apple puree until frothy. Stir in the dry ingredients. Pour into the prepared tin and gently swirl in the blueberry mixture.
6 Bake for 35–40 minutes until golden and cooked in the centre. Leave in the tin for 10 minutes to set then turn out and place onto a serving plate, right way up.
7 Pour the **Blueberry sauce** over the warm cake and serve with **Vanilla custard**.

Serves 8

BLUEBERRY SAUCE

Place the sugar, orange juice and half of the blueberries into a saucepan and stir over medium heat. Bring to the boil then reduce the heat and simmer until the berries release their juice. In a small bowl dissolve the cornflour in 1 teaspoon of the juice and stir back into the sauce. Simmer, stirring, for another few minutes until the sauce thickens. Remove from the heat, add the remaining blueberries and stir until heated through.

My gluten free kitchen

I've been into small corner stores that weren't as well provisioned as my kitchen and I have a friend who stares into my pantry in wonder, but a well stocked kitchen simply makes for an easier gluten free lifestyle.

White rice flour
Brown rice flour
Rice flour blend
Soy flour
Buckwheat flour
Potato starch
Tapioca flour
Pure maize cornflour (cornstarch)
Glutinous/sweet rice flour
Commercial gluten free plain
    (all-purpose) flour❖
Powdered milk

Pure icing (confectioners') sugar
Caster (superfine) sugar
Soft brown sugar
Maple syrup
Golden syrup
Hazelnut cocoa spread
Baking powder❖
Bicarbonate of soda (baking
    soda)
Xanthan gum
Unsweetened cocoa powder
Vanilla essence or extract
Ground cinnamon
Whole nutmeg
Allspice
Ground ginger
Cinnamon sticks
Vanilla beans

Poppadoms❖
Thin rice cakes

Round rice crackers
Rice Ring Cookies❖
Corn tortillas❖
Corn chips❖
Taco shells❖
Popping corn
Tannour Bread❖

Brown rice
Basmati rice
Wild blend rice
Risotto rice
Quinoa
Polenta
Sago
Rice stick noodles, dried
Rice sheets, dried, round
    or square
Dried pasta❖
Express Rice in a Cup❖
Coconut milk/cream

Tahini
Curry paste❖
Tomato paste (concentrated
    puree)
Crushed garlic, bottled
Crushed ginger, bottled
Crushed chilli, bottled
Tom Yum soup mix❖
Tomato soup❖
Chopped tomatoes, canned
Tomato passata (pureed
    tomatoes, bottled

Oyster sauce❖
Fish sauce❖
Soy sauce❖

Black olives
Roast capsicum (pepper),
    bottled
Marinated artichokes, bottled
Corn kernels, tinned
Cannellini beans, tinned
Adzuki beans, tinned
Chickpeas, tinned
Lentils, tinned

Chicken and vegetable stock❖
Baby capers
Tuna in oil
Red salmon
Dijon mustard❖
Grain mustard❖
Salsa, bottled❖
Pureed apples
Pureed apple and raspberries

Red wine vinegar
White wine vinegar
Cider vinegar
Olive oil
Canola oil
Macadamia oil

Puffed rice❖
Cornflakes❖
Rolled rice flakes

Protein powder❖
Soy Flakes❖
Pecan nuts
Almonds
Ground almonds
Pine nuts
Brazil nuts
Sultanas
Dried cranberries (craisins)
Dried dates

Cumin, ground
Coriander, ground
Sweet paprika
Sea salt
Black peppercorns
Pink peppercorns
Cayenne pepper, ground
Caraway seeds
Chinese five-spice
Garam masala
Cardamon, ground

In the refrigerator
Plain Greek style yoghurt
Feta cheese
Fresh parmesan cheese
Cheddar cheese
Large eggs
Blueberries, frozen
Raspberries, frozen
Gluten free bread, frozen❖
Pizza bases, frozen❖
Cheese bread balls, frozen❖

ACKNOWLEDGMENTS

Since being diagnosed with coeliac disease there have been a number of people and publications that have inspired me to continue making great food, despite the need to adapt to a gluten free diet. My best source of inspiration has been *Australian Gourmet Traveller* magazine. I was always an avid reader, but mostly of the travel section. I usually just skimmed through the food section, more to get an idea of what to order at the latest restaurants. Then all of a sudden I found that if I wanted to eat the same innovative food as before I had better learn to cook it myself, so I started spending a lot more time reading the food section. The simple and enlightened approach to fresh produce and promotion of Australian food producers and chefs showed me that just because I couldn't eat four particular ingredients, the list of possibilities was still endless — I just had to have a positive approach and apply a bit of lateral thinking.

My second inspiration has been the *Good Living* section of *The Sydney Morning Herald*, which opened my eyes to the dedicated food retailers and Growers Markets where the produce was always so beautiful and interesting that I was spoilt for choice. Even though I now live in Brisbane I never miss Tuesday's edition of *The Sydney Morning Herald*.

And thirdly, Stephanie Alexander — I constantly refer to her classic book, *Cook's Companion*, an inspired birthday gift from my family when I was still recovering my health.

The various contributions I received while writing this book, especially humour, patience and encouragement have been priceless. Many thanks go to: Dayle Moses, whose general enthusiasm for all things food was invaluable in getting this project off the ground: Libby Ginn, whose beautiful photos illustrate my recipes and with whom I had such a good time while we were shooting that my confidence soared: Jeff Palmer, who took me seriously as a self-publisher, explained the terminology — often twice — and cheerfully showed me the way to print a book: Natalie Sullivan, my neighbour and friend, who required all her professional training while I went on endlessly about 'the book' and whose lovely white plates feature in the photos.

Lastly, thank you to the many people who so generously gave me their precious time and expertise, especially Bruce Peebles, Jackie Passmore and Mike Holmes.

Robyn Russell

Index